ACCESS 2000
FOR WINDOWS®
FOR
DUMMIES®

Quick Reference

by Alison Barrows

Hungry Minds™

HUNGRY MINDS, INC.

New York, NY ◆ Cleveland, OH ◆ Indianapolis, IN

Access 2000 For Windows® For Dummies® Quick Reference

Published by
Hungry Minds, Inc.
909 Third Avenue
New York, NY 10022
www.hungryminds.com

Library of Congress Catalog Card No.: 99-61123

ISBN: 0-7645-0445-2

Printed in the United States of America

10 9 8 7 6 5 4 3

1O/QW/QU/QR/IN

Distributed in the United States by Hungry Minds, Inc.

Distributed by CDG Books Canada Inc. for Canada; by Transworld Publishers Limited in the United Kingdom; by IDG Norge Books for Norway; by IDG Sweden Books for Sweden; by IDG Books Australia Publishing Corporation Pty. Ltd. for Australia and New Zealand; by TransQuest Publishers Pte Ltd. for Singapore, Malaysia, Thailand, Indonesia, and Hong Kong; by Gotop Information Inc. for Taiwan; by ICG Muse, Inc. for Japan; by Intersoft for South Africa; by Eyrolles for France; by International Thomson Publishing for Germany, Austria and Switzerland; by Distribuidora Cuspide for Argentina; by LR International for Brazil; by Galileo Libros for Chile; by Ediciones ZETA S.C.R. Ltda. for Peru; by WS Computer Publishing Corporation, Inc., for the Philippines; by Contemporanea de Ediciones for Venezuela; by Express Computer Distributors for the Caribbean and West Indies; by Micronesia Media Distributor, Inc. for Micronesia; by Chips Computadoras S.A. de C.V. for Mexico; by Editorial Norma de Panama S.A. for Panama; by American Bookshops for Finland.

For general information on Hungry Minds' products and services please contact our Customer Care Department within the U.S. at 800-762-2974, outside the U.S. at 317-572-3993 or fax 317-572-4002.

For sales inquiries and reseller information, including discounts, premium and bulk quantity sales, and foreign-language translations, please contact our Customer Care Department at 800-434-3422, fax 317-572-4002, or write to Hungry Minds, Inc., Attn: Customer Care Department, 10475 Crosspoint Boulevard, Indianapolis, IN 46256.

For information on licensing foreign or domestic rights, please contact our Sub-Rights Customer Care Department at 650-653-7098.

For information on using Hungry Minds' products and services in the classroom or for ordering examination copies, please contact our Educational Sales Department at 800-434-2086 or fax 317-572-4005.

Please contact our Public Relations Department at 212-884-5163 for press review copies or 212-884-5000 for author interviews and other publicity information or fax 212-884-5400.

For authorization to photocopy items for corporate, personal, or educational use, please contact Copyright Clearance Center, 222 Rosewood Drive, Danvers, MA 01923, or fax 978-750-4470.

Hungry Minds™ is a trademark of Hungry Minds, Inc.

About the Author

Alison Barrows has taken the long route to ...*For Dummies* writing, most recently thinking she would have a career in economics. A serious computer user since high school, she found herself irresistibly drawn into technical support, training, and documentation with help from friends who are ...*For Dummies* authors.

Since finding herself in a career as a writer, Alison has authored or coauthored seven books for IDG Books including *Dummies 101: WordPerfect 8* and *Excel 97 Secrets*. During her career in technical writing and training, she has designed and written software courses and taught hundreds of computer users how to make computers work for them. In addition to writing books, Alison teaches custom computer courses and writes technical documentation and training material.

Alison has a master's degree in Public Policy from the Kennedy School at Harvard University and a B.A. from Wellesley College. In real life, she loves to sing, watch *Star Trek* (the newer versions), cook, and dabble in yoga, rock climbing, and Ultimate Frisbee. She currently lives in Boylston, Massachusetts, with her husband, Matt, and the newest member of the family, their Portuguese Water Dog puppy Jake.

Dedication

To Jake, in honor of his rebooting.

Author's Acknowledgments

I'd like to thank Margy Levine Young and John Levine for moral support and for getting me into this terrific business.

I could never get my work done if it weren't for Matt (also known as "Honey") providing around-the-clock moral support and keeping the computers in such a state that I can actually get work done.

I'd also like to thank Colleen Esterline, my Project Editor, for keeping her finger on the pulse of this book while she was also getting married and moving halfway across the country. Kathleen Dobie did an excellent and tactful job of copy editing.

I'd also like to acknowledge TIAC and IECC, my almost flawless Internet and e-mail providers.

Publisher's Acknowledgments

We're proud of this book; please send us your comments through our Hungry Minds Online Registration Form located at: www.dummies.com.

Some of the people who helped bring this book to market include the following:

Acquisitions, Editorial, and Media Development

Project Editor:
Colleen Williams Esterline

Acquisitions Editor: Steven H. Hayes

Copy Editor: Kathleen Dobie

Technical Editor: Allen Wyatt, Discovery Computing, Inc.

Editorial Manager: Mary Corder

Production

Project Coordinator: Valery Bourke

Layout and Graphics: Linda M. Boyer, J. Tyler Connor, Angela F. Hunckler, Drew R. Moore, Brent Savage, M. Anne Sipahimalani, Kate Snell, Michael A. Sullivan

Proofreaders: Christine Berman, Kelli Botta, Joel K. Draper, Jennifer Mahern, Nancy Price, Ethel M. Winslow

Indexer: Sherry Massey

Special Help

Suzanne Thomas, Christine Meloy Beck

General and Administrative

Hungry Minds, Inc.: John Kilcullen, CEO; Bill Barry, President and COO; John Ball, Executive VP, Operations & Administration; John Harris, CFO

Hungry Minds Technology Publishing Group: Richard Swadley, Senior Vice President and Publisher; Mary Bednarek, Vice President and Publisher, Networking and Certification; Walter R. Bruce III, Vice President and Publisher, General User and Design Professional; Joseph Wikert, Vice President and Publisher, Programming; Mary C. Corder, Editorial Director, Branded Technology Editorial; Andy Cummings, Publishing Director, General User and Design Professional; Barry Pruett, Publishing Director, Visual

Hungry Minds Manufacturing: Ivor Parker, Vice President, Manufacturing

Hungry Minds Marketing: John Helmus, Assistant Vice President, Director of Marketing

Hungry Minds Online Management: Brenda McLaughlin, Executive Vice President, Chief Internet Officer

Hungry Minds Production for Branded Press: Debbie Stailey, Production Director

Hungry Minds Sales: Roland Elgey, Senior Vice President, Sales and Marketing; Michael Violano, Vice President, International Sales and Sub Rights

♦

The publisher would like to give special thanks to Patrick J. McGovern, without whom this book would not have been possible.

♦

Contents at a Glance

Table of Contents

How to Use This Book

If you're looking for a book that fits neatly beside your monitor and gives you easy access to short and useful descriptions of how to get your work done, then this is the book for you. *Access 2000 For Windows For Dummies Quick Reference* is a great book to have when all you want is a reference — not the nitty-gritty *why* and *why not.* This little book doesn't take up space telling you *why* you need to do something, but it's a great place to find out how to do a task.

In this book, you can find loads of step-by-step instructions organized alphabetically by topic. If you already know what you need to find, look it up alphabetically in the appropriate part. If you can't find what you need, check the Index or the Table of Contents. If you just want to know more about some aspect of Access, flip through a part or two and read the topics that look unfamiliar to you. You may discover tricks and tips you didn't even know existed!

This is not the book to use when you're building a database from scratch and you don't know where to start. For that situation, you need a more comprehensive book — one that shows you the ins and outs of building a new database. For such in-depth information, pick up a copy of *Access 2000 For Windows For Dummies*, by John Kaufeld, or *Access 2000 Bible* by Cary Prague and Michael Irwin (both from IDG Books Worldwide, Inc.).

How This Book Is Organized

This book covers beginning and intermediate skills, and (to a lesser extent) advanced skills. You won't find hard-core Access programming stuff here, such as setting up menu-based MIS systems and programming Access using VBA. You will find specific instructions on how to get your daily work done in Access.

The book is broken into eight parts, each dealing with a specific aspect of Access.

Part I: Access Basics

Part I introduces the basics — the things you really need to know before you can get much done in Access. Starting Access, closing Access, opening a database, and getting help are all covered in this part. You can also find information on the Access screen, how to work with windows, and some general pointers on using those wonderful Access wizards.

Part I is the only part that's not alphabetized. Instead, this part presents some basic Access 2000 skills in a logical order. If you're looking for tips on getting started with Access 2000, you may want to go through Part I from start to finish, just to get yourself headed in the right direction.

Part II: Creating and Navigating a Database

Part II covers the specifics of creating a new database and finding your way around a database that you already have.

Part III: Tables: A Home for Your Data

Part III describes all the nitty-gritty tasks you need to know to create tables and put data into them. You'll also find information on linking tables through the Relationships window in this part. Turn to this part to find out how to define fields, enter and edit data, and work in the table Datasheet and Design views. You will also discover more about data types and how to use input masks and validation rules to limit the data that can be entered in a field.

Part IV: Queries: Getting Answers from Your Data

Part IV deals with all the details you need to know to use queries to get the answers you need from your data. Queries are great for displaying related information from different tables or for finding specific data that meets certain criteria you set. You can also use queries to create aggregate calculations: Want to know how many orders you receive in a week? A query can give you the answer.

Part V: Reporting Results

Part V covers everything you need to know about reports. Reports are the best Access tool for putting your results on paper. Reports enable you to group and sort data. You can even create a report for a query or a filtered table.

Most of the work you do on a report takes place in Report Design view. This part tells you how to use Report Design view to create sections in a report, put text and lines on the report, and display the contents of fields. Much of the material in this part about using the report Design view you'll also find useful when you're creating forms in Design view.

Part VI: Forms and Data Access Pages for Displaying and Entering Data

Forms are a great way to enter data. They enable you to create on-screen something like a paper form that you may use to record information with a pen. By using an Access form, you can display only relevant fields. You can even create check boxes and drop-down lists to ease data entry.

Data Access Pages are a new feature in Access 2000. They allow you to use Access to create an HTML page (a Web page) that can be used to enter or display data.

Part VII: Printing Your Work for the World to See

You can print any object in an Access database. Whatever you print, this part arms you with the skills you need — such as how to preview before you print, how to change the page layout, and how to print only specific pages.

Part VIII: Access 2000 Tips and Tricks

This part contains some of the miscellaneous useful topics that don't fit into another part. In this part, you can find details on cutting and pasting, checking the spelling of your data, sharing your Access data, and using data stored in other applications. The most important topic in this part is information about how to back up your database.

Conventions Used in This Book

The directions in this book often include a menu command. Such commands appear like this:

Choose File⇨Open.

This sentence tells you to click the File option on the main menu and then click Open from the drop-down menu.

You can also choose menu commands by using the hotkeys, the underlined letters in the command. First press the Alt key to make the menu active and then type the underlined letters to choose the menu item.

The directions in this book may also tell you to type something:

Things you should type appear in bold.

You can may run into messages that your computer is sending to you:

```
Computer messages look like this.
```

Occasionally, the text refers to a generic table or field name. The generic name will appear in italics. So if you see *TableName.* * in the book, you should look for the name of an actual table in your database, followed by a period and an asterisk on your screen.

Icons Used in This Book

What's a computer book without icons to help show you the way? The following icons appear in this book:

This icon signals a good way to do something, often a method you may not have considered.

This icon flags the quickest way to complete a task.

This icon points out a feature that doesn't work exactly as you may expect it to.

This icon steers you clear of pitfalls that could be harmful to you, your computer, or your data.

This icon refers to another IDG Books Worldwide book for more information about the task at hand.

This icon points out features that are new in Access 2000.

Getting to Know Access 2000

Part I provides some basic database concepts as well as a quick overview of what you need to know about Windows to use Access 2000. This part covers some fundamental definitions, such as what a database is and what its most important pieces are. Look here for a review of the parts of the Access screen and for information on how to open, save, and close database files. This part also covers how to get online help, including how to use that cute little animated character, the Office Assistant.

In this part...

✔ **Defining a database**

✔ **Getting started in Access 2000**

✔ **Naming the parts of the screen**

✔ **Reading the menus**

✔ **Using dialog boxes**

✔ **Opening, saving, and closing an Access file**

✔ **Getting Help with Access**

✔ **Closing Access 2000**

About Databases

A *database* is an organized collection of related data. In a well-built database, you can organize your data so that you see only the data you need to see, in the order you need to see it. In technical terms, a database enables you to *filter* and *sort* data. You can also choose the format in which you want to view your data — a table, for example, or a form.

On the most basic level, databases are organized into records. A *record* is one batch of related information. If you think of your address book as a database, one record is the information about your best friend — her name, address, phone number, and any other information that you have about her in the address book.

Tables store records of data. A table consists of rows and columns. The rows are records, and the columns are fields. A *field* is one category of information that you collect for every record. In a database that stores your address book, the fields may be first name, last name, street address, birthday, and so on.

First Name	Last Name	Street	City	State	Zip
Emma	Rucci	322 Apple Ave.	Norway	ME	04268
Nora	Sweeney	95 Lilly Ave.	Canaan	VT	05903
Edward	Dill	817 Tulip Ave.	Belgrade	ME	04917
Jake	Barrows	9569 Crocus Rd.	South China	ME	04358
Madeline	Molkenbur	15 Hydrangea St.	Poland	ME	04358
Zeke	Mace	456 Iris St.	Jericho	VT	05465
Riley	Newman	76 Peony Rd.	Naples	ME	04055
Figaro	Aronoff	149 Rose Ave.	Lisbon	ME	04250
Fennel	Smith	5 Raspberry St.	Orleans	MA	02653
Seth	Ronn	116 Tuberose Rd.	New Britain	CT	06050
Abby	Aikens	11448 Orchard La.	New Sweden	ME	04762
Farley	Spitzer	26 Meadow La.	Mexico	ME	04257
Jillian	Staiti	48 Cotton Candy Rd.	Belfast	ME	04915
Bjorn	Marik	748 Phlox St.	Jamaica	VT	05343

Record: 1 of 17

It's important to store each type of information in a separate field. Organizing your data into many different fields enables you to slice the data any way you want. For instance, if you decide that having separate fields for first and last names is a waste of time, you lose out on the option of sorting the database by either first or last name.

Access is a *relational database,* which means that one database file can consist of many tables of *related* data. For example, you may have a table called Orders that lists orders and includes the Product Number of each item ordered, and another table called Products that contains information about products, which identifies each product using another Product Number field. When you tell Access that the two Product Number fields are related, you provide a link between the two tables that allows you to ask your database a question that requires data from both tables to answer. For instance, you may want to know who ordered which products (information stored in the Orders table) and how much the product costs at wholesale (information stored in the Products table). The related Product Number fields allow you to pull the related data from two tables.

See also "Relating (Linking) Tables," in Part II for more information on relating tables.

Access Database Objects

An Access database can contain different types of Access *objects:* tables, forms, queries, and reports.

✦ Access stores data in *tables.*

✦ You use Access *forms* just like paper forms: to enter and display data.

✦ You create *queries* to gather the information you need about the data you've entered.

✦ Use *reports* to present the information you gather about your data.

Each of these types of objects is covered in a part of this book.

Starting Access 2000

Windows almost always gives you more than one way to perform a task, and starting Access is no exception. The most popular way to start Access is to use the Start button in the taskbar.

Some of the ways to start Access, including the Start-button method, follow:

✦ Click the Start button and choose Programs⇨Microsoft Access. (You may have to highlight the Microsoft Office option in order to see and click Microsoft Access.)

✦ If you have the Microsoft Office shortcut bar, click the Open a Document button on it, choose an existing Access database, and click the Open button.

✦ Double-click an existing Access database file in Windows Explorer or My Computer. Windows starts Access and opens the database that you double-clicked.

To read about more ways to open any Windows program, get a book about Windows, such as *Windows 98 For Dummies,* by Andy Rathbone (IDG Books Worldwide, Inc.).

Access Menus and Buttons

 A new feature of Access 2000 hides infrequently used commands on the menu. A double arrow at the bottom of a drop-down menu indicates that all the menu options are not displayed.

To see the whole menu, select the double arrow or just wait — if you keep the mouse pointer still for a couple of seconds on an open menu, the whole menu appears automatically.

Some buttons in Access work like menus. When you see an arrow to the right of a button, you have two choices: You can click the button to perform whatever action the button does, or you can click the arrow to choose from a group of similar actions.

The icon for one of the options on the drop-down list matches the icon on the button. Clicking the button performs the task listed next to the matching icon. The New Object button creates an AutoForm unless you use the drop-down list to choose another kind of object to create. (AutoForm automatically creates a form using the fields in the selected table or query.) Drop-down menus on buttons may also have the double-arrow at the bottom that indicates that items on the menu are missing — for these you have to select the double arrow to see all the menu choices.

See also "Creating a Form with an AutoForm," in Part VI for more information about AutoForms.

Opening a Database File

When you start Access by using the Start⇨Programs menu, a dialog box lists databases that you've used recently. To open one of these databases, select it from this initial dialog box (be sure that the Open an Existing File option is selected), and click OK.

You can also open an Access file by double-clicking the filename in Windows Explorer or My Computer, or by choosing the file off of the Start⇨Documents menu. Opening an Access file also starts Access.

If you're already in Access, use the Open dialog box to open a file, or choose a recently used database file from the bottom of the File menu.

Follow these steps to use the Open dialog box to open a database:

1. Click the Open button. (Alternatively, choose File⇨Open or press Ctrl+O.)

Another way to display the Open dialog box is to select the More Files option from the dialog box that appears when you first start Access, and then click OK.

2. Select the file you want. (You may need to browse to it.) Use the icons on the left of the Open dialog box to see different folders — History displays recently used files, Desktop displays desktop icons, Favorites displays the contents of the Favorites folder, and Web Folders displays defined Web folders. *See also* Part VII for more information about the Web Folders option.

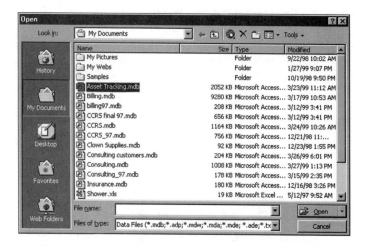

3. Click the Open button or simply double-click the filename. Access opens the database.

Make sure that the Files of Type list box shows the type of file you want to open — usually Microsoft Access Databases (*.mdb) or All Files (*.*). The Files of Type control limits the files that appear in the Open dialog box, so depending on the option selected, some files may not be listed.

If you recently used the Access database file that you want to open now, you can start Access and open the database by choosing the file from the Documents menu in the Start menu, which lists the last few files that you used. Click the Start button, choose Documents, and click the file you want to open. If you're already in Access, you can choose a recently used file from the bottom of the Access File menu.

Saving a Database File

Access is designed so that many people can use one database — and all at the same time, if they need to. So, unlike a spreadsheet or word processing program, Access doesn't require you to save the entire file — instead you save object definitions (such as a table or form definition) one at a time. Access takes care of saving data as soon as it's entered.

 To save an object definition, make the object active (by clicking its window) and then click the Save button on the toolbar, or press Ctrl+S, or choose File⇨Save. If you close an object without saving it, Access displays a dialog box asking whether you want to save the object:

✦ Choose Yes to save the object.

✦ Choose No to close the object without saving changes to the definition.

✦ Choose Cancel to cancel the command and return to the unsaved object.

Converting to a prior version

 Access 2000 saves database files in a new format that is incompatible with prior versions of Access. If you are sharing a database with someone who is not using Access 2000, the easiest way to share the database is to convert it to a format they can use. A more complicated alternative (briefly covered at the end of this section) is to create a front-end/back-end application that allows you to use the advanced features in Access 2000 while still allowing users with older versions of Access to use the database.

Follow these steps to save the database in an earlier format:

1. Open the database you want to convert.

2. Choose Tools⇨Database Utilities⇨Convert Database⇨To Prior Access Database Version.

3. Name the converted database using the File Name field.

4. Click the Save button.

The new database is Access 97 compatible.

To create a front-end/back-end application, use the Database Splitter wizard to create an SQL Server database and a Microsoft Access project. In order to do this, you must have Microsoft SQL

Server installed on a computer where you can store the database. The project file is stored in any location, but usually a local hard drive. To access the wizard, choose Tools⇨Database Utilities⇨ Database Splitter.

Compacting and repairing a database

Access does not automatically compact a database when you close it. However, if you have any problems with a database such as slower than usual response or frequent errors, you may want to try compacting and repairing it. To compact and repair the open database, choose Tools⇨Database Utilities⇨Compact and Repair Database.

Closing a Database File

To close a database, simply close the database window by clicking its Close (X) button. The database window is the window that has `Name of the database file: Database` in the title bar.

Working with Wizards

Access provides wizards to help you build and use databases. A *wizard* consists of a series of dialog boxes that ask you questions and then creates something (such as a database, a query, or a report) based on your answers. The many wizards in Access 2000 do a variety of tasks, but they all work in a similar way: They present you with screens that ask you questions, such as which tables or fields you want to use and which format you prefer.

I cover specific wizards in other parts of this book, but the following sections cover the basic techniques you must know in order to use any wizard.

Selecting fields

Many wizards have windows like the following one, where you choose fields.

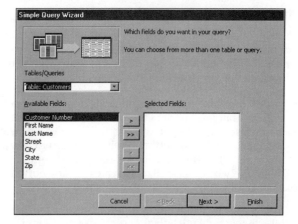

To tell Access that you want to use a field, you first have to tell it where to find the field by choosing a table or query from the drop-down list in the Tables/Queries list box. Access displays the fields from the table or query you choose in the Available Fields list box. Use one of the following methods to tell Access that you want it to use a field:

♦ Double-click the field.

♦ Select the field and click the single right-facing arrow button.

To choose all the fields displayed in the Available Fields list box, click the double right-facing arrow.

If you make a mistake, and want to remove a field from the Selected Fields list box, double-click it, or select it and click the single left-facing arrow button.

To remove all fields from the Selected Fields list box, click the double left-facing arrow button.

To select fields from other tables or queries, choose another table or query from the Tables/Queries drop-down list and select the additional fields.

Viewing more windows

When you finish answering all the questions on one window of a wizard, you're ready to see the next window. The buttons at the bottom of the wizard enable you to proceed through the questions the wizard asks you:

♦ **Cancel:** Exits the wizard without letting the wizard complete its task.

♦ **Back:** Displays the previous window of the wizard.

◆ **Next:** Displays the next window of the wizard.

◆ **Finish:** Tells Access to complete whatever it is that this particular wizard does, using the information it already has, and using the default values on any windows that you skip by clicking the Finish button.

Every wizard has information that it needs in order to work, and other settings that are optional (if you don't change them, Access uses a default setting). As you work through the wizard, you can choose to click the Finish button to tell the wizard to complete its task, or you can click the Next button to see more options. If you click Finish, the wizard uses default values for any options you choose not to change.

When you get to the last window of a wizard, you see the black and white checkered Finish flag. Access asks you if you want help, and it often asks you to name the object the wizard is creating and choose how you want to view the new object. When you finish with these options, click the Finish button to tell the wizard to complete its task.

Getting Help

Access offers you help in several ways. You can use the Office Assistant or the online Help system. Both methods tap into the same information; the difference is in the way you find the information. For help with a particular setting, you may find a Screen Tip useful. For more advanced help, you may want the Developers Solutions database.

Microsoft also offers Office on the Web help, which is also accessed through the Help menu. Office on the Web offers product updates.

Online help

To get online help, press F1 or choose Help⇨Microsoft Access Help. Access displays the Office Assistant if the Office Assistant is turned on. Otherwise you see the Microsoft Access Help window.

Help information

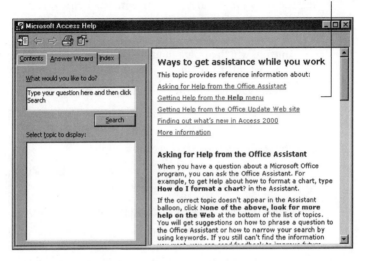

The Microsoft Access Help window has three tabs that guide you to the different types of help that you may need:

✦ **Contents:** Displays a list of help topics (like a manual). Double-click topics that have a book in front of them to display subtopics. Double-click topics that have a question mark to display an actual help screen.

✦ **Answer Wizard:** Allows you to ask a question. The Help system provides topics for you to choose from.

✦ **Index:** Displays an index of topics covered in the Help system. Type the first few letters of the topic that you're looking for in the first box. Choose the topic you want to view by double-clicking it or by selecting it and then clicking the Display button.

The Help window also provides some tools that you can use: buttons, links, and windows that pop up when you click particular words or symbols.

The buttons at the top of the Help window are useful for navigating the Help system and working with the help you find:

✦ **Hide:** Displays the Help pane and hides the pane with the Contents, Answer Wizard, and Index tabs. Click the Show button, which appears in the same position, to redisplay the pane with the Contents, Answer Wizard, and Index tabs.

✦ **Back:** Displays the previous Help topic.

✦ **Forward:** Displays the next Help topic. This button is only active if you have used the Back button.

✦ **Print:** Prints the displayed Help topic.

✦ **Options:** Displays a drop-down list of options — things that you can do with Help windows.

Close the Help window by clicking its Close (X) button.

Unless you've changed the default setting, when you press F1, the Office Assistant appears. If you find the Office Assistant a little annoying and prefer to see the Microsoft Access Help window when you press F1, display the Office Assistant, click the Options button, and remove the check mark from the Use the Office Assistant option.

What's This?

You can get context sensitive help on a displayed Access option by using the What's This? option on the Help menu. Choose Help➪ What's This, then click the item you want more information about. The Microsoft Access Help window will open and display help about the clicked item.

The Office Assistant

Access 2000 offers you help in the form of the Office Assistant, an animated paper clip. When the Office Assistant is visible it may offer you help with the task you are performing. It tries to amuse you with animation when the computer is doing something (such as saving a file).

When you have a question, you can click the Office Assistant. It will display help topics that may be useful to you based on the window you are working in or the position of the cursor. To view help on the topic, click the topic. If none of the topics provides the information you need, type a question into the Office Assistant and press Enter. The list of suggested help topics is revised, and often the last option is See More, which, when clicked, displays more help topics.

Here's how to work with the Office Assistant:

✦ You can close the Office Assistant by right-clicking the icon and choosing Hide.

✦ If you've hidden the Office Assistant and want it redisplayed, click the Office Assistant button on the toolbar or anywhere else you see it (it appears in some dialog boxes), or press F1. You may need to choose Help⇨Show the Office Assistant if you've hidden the Office Assistant more permanently.

✦ If you want help, click the Office Assistant; type your question in the white box; and then press Enter or click Search. The Office Assistant suggests some topics that may be what you're looking for. Click the topic or the light bulb next to the topic to display the Help window on the topic.

✦ Choose a different Office Assistant (it doesn't have to look like a paper clip — it can be a bouncing smiley face or an Einstein figurine, among other choices) by right-clicking the Office Assistant, choosing Choose Assistant, clicking the Gallery tab, and following the directions in the dialog box.

✦ Change the way the Office Assistant works by right-clicking it, choosing Options, and changing settings in the Options tab. The settings let you tell the Office Assistant the kind of help you want to see.

✦ Move the Office Assistant out of the way by clicking and dragging it.

Screen tips

Screen tips help you with menu options and dialog box controls. To see a screen tip, use one of the following methods.

✦ Press Shift+F1 when the option you want information on is highlighted.

✦ Click the ? button on the dialog box, and then click the option you want information on (not all dialog boxes have the ? button).

Sample databases

Access comes with a number of samples that can help you understand how Access databases work.

The Northwind database is the most frequently used sample database. The database is an example of how to track products, suppliers, and sales for a company called Northwind Traders. Playing around with the Northwind database is one way to become familiar with different Access features.

The Northwind database is stored in C:\Program Files\Microsoft Office\Office\Samples\Nwind.mdb when it is installed. If it has not been installed, it can be found on your Access 2000 or Office 2000 CD in /Pfiles/Msoffice/Office/Samples.

See also "Using other Access Resources," in Part VIII.

Help on the Web

Access 2000 contains an additional source of help — a Web site set up specifically to provide updates and help that were not available when the version of the software you own shipped. To access help on the Web, choose Help⇨Office on the Web.

Many non-Microsoft Web sites also offer Access information. Use your favorite search engine to search for Microsoft Access.

Quitting Access 2000

You quit Access the same way that you quit any other Windows program. Once again, Windows offers a boatload of options. If you have parts of a database open, and you've made changes since the last time you saved the object, Access gives you the option of saving the object before you quit.

Following are the most popular ways to close Access:

+ Click the Close button in the top-right corner of the Access window (it looks like an X).

+ Double-click the Access window's properties box in the top-left corner of the window. (Alternatively, click the properties box and then choose Close from the drop-down menu.)

+ Choose File⇨Exit from the Access menu.

+ Press Alt+F4 when Access is the active window.

Part II

Creating and Navigating a Database

You can choose between two approaches to create a new database — you can start from scratch, or you can use a wizard. This part covers both methods.

After you create a database, or when you need to use one that someone else created, you have to know how to get around it — and that means knowing how to use the Database window.

In this part . . .

✔ Creating a database from scratch

✔ Using a wizard to create a database

✔ Using the Database window

✔ Navigating your database

✔ Creating relationships between tables

Creating a Database

Designing databases is a topic unto itself — this little Quick Reference certainly can't tell you everything you need to know. For more guidance on how to design a database, see *Access 2000 For Windows For Dummies* by John Kaufeld (IDG Books Worldwide, Inc.), or *Microsoft Access 2000 Bible,* by Cary Prague and Michael Irwin (IDG Books Worldwide, Inc.).

I can, however, give you some basic guidelines. It is important to give some consideration to the design of your database before you begin entering data into tables. Consider the data you have and how you want to use it — what kinds of queries, forms, and reports do you want to include in your database? What additional needs may crop up later? These questions help you figure out what data you need, and how to break up your data into fields and tables so that you can create the reports, forms, and queries that you will need.

Much of the work of designing a database to meet your needs is in deciding how to break your data into fields and which fields to store in each table; these can make or break your database. Use these guidelines for designing your database:

✦ Split data into its smallest logical parts. Usually this means the smallest unit that you may ever want to use. For instance, give each name at least two fields: first name and last name. This allows you to work with either one or the other for sorting, form letters, and so on.

✦ Use multiple tables so that each table contains information on one topic. For instance, one table may contain order information, while another contains the customer's billing information and shipping address. You can password-protect a table, so it makes sense to put sensitive information in a separate table.

✦ Make sure you know which fields in different tables are related. For instance, the Customer Number field you use in the Orders table connects to the Customer Number in the Customer table containing customer's shipping addresses and billing information.

✦ Avoid repeating data. If a table listing employee information has fields for both department name and department manager you are repeating data. It may make more sense to list a department in the employee table and have a separate table for departments and department managers.

If you're designing a complex database, consider consulting a reference that gives more detail on designing databases such as *Microsoft Access 2000 Bible,* by Cary N. Prague and Michael R. Irwin (IDG Books Worldwide, Inc.).

Developing a database

Follow these general steps to develop a database:

1. Open a new database.

2. Create tables. See the guidelines in the previous section on designing your tables so that they contain data in a way that will be useful to you.

   See also "Creating a Table," in Part III for more information.

3. Tell Access how your tables are related.

   See also "Relating (Linking) Tables," in Part III for more information.

4. (Optional) Create forms to make data entry clearer and to display a full record's worth of information at a time.

   See also "Adding a Form to Your Database," in Part VI for more information.

5. Enter your data.

   See also "Adding Data to your Database," in Part III and "Entering Data Through a Form," in Part VI for more information.

6. Create queries to give you the information you need.

   See also "Adding a Select Query to the Database," in Part IV.

7. Create reports to transfer the information to paper in a clear format.

   See also "Adding a New Report to Your Database," in Part V.

Creating a database from scratch

You can create an empty database in the following ways:

✦ If Access is closed, you have two options:

   • Start Access by using the Start button menu (or your favorite method) and, in the introductory dialog box, choose Blank Access Database. Access displays the File New Database dialog box, where you name the new database.

- Choose New Office Document from the Start button menu (or click the New Office Document button in the Microsoft Office shortcut bar). You see the New Office Document dialog box with multiple tabs at the top. Click the General tab, select the Blank Database icon, and click OK. (The Databases tab contains icons for all the database wizards.)

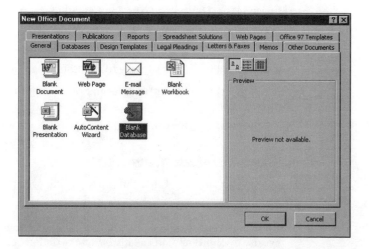

✦ If Access is running, click the New Database button, press Alt+N, or choose File⇨New Database. The New dialog box appears. Click the General tab in the New dialog box, select Blank Database, and then click OK. Access displays the File New Database dialog box with the File Name setting highlighted.

Use this dialog box to give the database a filename by typing the name of the new database into the File Name box. If you want to store the file in a folder other than the one displayed in the Save In box, change the folder. Then click Create.

Access takes a few seconds to create the new database; then it displays the Tables view of the Database window and the Database toolbar.

 Access 2000 offers you a several new options on the New dialog box. You can create a new database, but you can also create a Data Access Page, a Project (using an existing database), and a Project using a new database.

See also Part VII for more about Data Access Pages. Projects are the way Microsoft has implemented Access as a front end to SQL Server databases. A project file contains only database objects that do not contain data — forms, reports, pages, macros, and modules. Tables, data, stored procedures, and database diagrams are stored in the SQL Server database. The process of working with the project is very similar to the process of working with the database, however the data is stored in the underlying SQL Server database and can be manipulated using the more complex SQL functions.

Creating a database with a wizard

 Using wizards is a great way to get a jumpstart on creating a database. Even if they don't provide exactly what you want, wizards give you a framework to start from.

See also "Working with Wizards," in Part I.

Access 2000 comes with a number of database wizards:

Asset Tracking	Ledger
Contact Management	Order Entry
Event Management	Resource Scheduling
Expenses	Service Call Management
Inventory Control	Time and Billing

Follow these steps to create a database by using a wizard:

 1. Display the New dialog box by choosing <u>D</u>atabase Wizard in the initial screen when you open Access and clicking OK, choosing <u>F</u>ile⇨<u>N</u>ew from the menu, clicking the New File button, or pressing Ctrl+N.

Access displays the New dialog box.

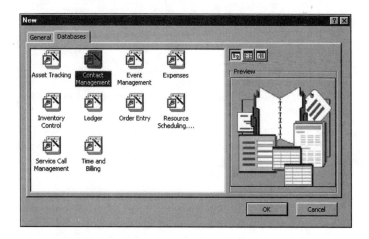

2. Click the Databases tab.

A list of wizards appears. The name of the wizard gives you a general idea about what kind of data the wizard is set up to work with.

3. Click a database name to get a graphical preview of the wizard.

4. To open a wizard, double-click the database icon (or name), or click the icon once to select it and then click the OK button.

Access displays the File New Database dialog box where you can name the database.

5. Accept the name in the File Name box by pressing Enter, or edit the name and then press Enter.

6. The wizard takes a few moments to set up, and then displays the first window, which shows you some information about the database that you're setting up. Click Next to display the next window of the wizard.

Click the Finish button now to accept the wizard's defaults and create the database.

7. Use the options on each window of the wizard to customize the database the wizard is creating for you. You may see more than one screen of options. Follow the directions in each screen to determine which options to change. Access allows you to add additional fields, choose a form style, choose a report style, and give the database a name (which will appear in the Access title bar). The last screen gives you a setting to check if you want to view online help about the database.

8. Click the Finish button to tell the wizard to create the database.

Finally, the database opens, displaying the Main Switchboard — a menu of options.

9. You can work with the database by using the menu, or you can display the familiar Database window by clicking the Database Window button. Redisplay the Main Switchboard by choosing it from the Window menu. You can also view the Switchboard by clicking the Forms button in the Database window and double-clicking Switchboard.

Finding Your Way Around a Database

An Access database consists of data and database objects. Tables, reports, forms, and queries are the types of objects that you're most likely to work with. You may also work with macros and modules.

See also "Access Database Objects," in Part I.

The Database window is the table of contents for all the objects in your database. From the Database window you can access each object in the database.

Buttons for each type of object in the database

The Database window has a different look in Access 2000 than in prior versions of the software — object types appear as buttons on the left side of the window rather than as tabs across the top. You may notice the Database window now resembles Microsoft Outlook.

The view for each type of object contains at least two different types of icons — icons for creating a new object of this type, and icons for each defined object of this type in the database. For instance, in addition to the three tables defined in the database, you also see three icons for creating new tables (see the preceding figure). Notice that the icons for the tables and the icons that create new tables are different.

To see all the objects of a certain type, click the appropriate button. To see the names of all the forms in the database, for example, click the Forms button. To open a specific form, click the form name to select it and then click the Open button on the toolbar.

Use any of these ways to view the Database window:

◆ Click the Database Window button.

◆ Press F11.

◆ Choose Window from the menu and choose the item at the bottom of the drop-down menu that shows Name of Database: Database.

◆ If you can see even part of the Database window, click it to make it the active window.

Use the Database window to see any object in the database, or to create a new object. Click any button in the Objects list to see all the objects of that type. Click the Reports button, for example, to see all the reports in the database. You can then use the Open and Design buttons (or the Preview and Design buttons) in the Database window to view the selected object.

(Design view enables you to change the definition of the object. *See also* Parts III, IV, V, and VI for more information about using Design view for tables, queries, reports, and forms.)

The Database window toolbar

The Database window contains buttons useful for copying, printing, and creating objects. Here's the rundown on those buttons:

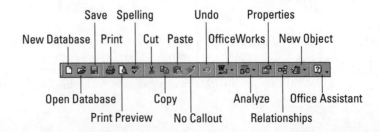

Button	What It Does
New Database	Creates a new database
Open Database	Opens an existing database (and closes the currently open database)
Print	Prints the selected object
Print Preview	Displays the selected object as it will look when printed
Spelling	Checks the spelling of the selected object
Cut	Deletes the selected object and saves a copy in the Windows Clipboard
Copy	Copies the selected object to the Windows Clipboard
Paste	Pastes the contents of the Windows Clipboard to the Database window
Undo	Undoes the last undoable action
OfficeLinks: Word	Opens another Office 2000 application
Analyze	Runs the Table Analyzer Wizard or another analyzer wizard
Properties	Displays the properties of the selected object
Relationships	Displays the Relationships window
New Object: Autoform	Creates a new object
Office Assistant	Displays the Office Assistant

In addition, the Database window has a secondary toolbar that contains these buttons:

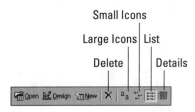

Button	What It Does
Open or Preview	Displays the selected object
Design	Displays the Design view of the selected object
New	Displays a dialog of options for creating a new object of the type currently displayed
Delete	Deletes the selected object
Large Icons	Displays objects in the Database window as large icons

(continued)

(continued)

Button	What It Does
Small Icons	Displays objects in the Database window as small icons
List	Displays objects in the Database window in a list
Details	Displays objects in the Database window with details, including a description, last date modified, date created, and type of object

One advantage of using the Details view is that you can see when an object was last modified. You can also sort objects — just click the gray column header to sort by that column. And, if you want to see which table was modified most recently, click the Modified column header.

Changing the name of an object

Access now takes care of all the complications that used to be caused by changing the name of a field or database object. When you change a name within the database, Access now finds references to the old name and updates them to the new name. However, in order for this to work, you must have permission to change all the necessary objects — in other words, if security features are used to prevent changes, the automatic name change throughout the database will not work.

Name AutoCorrect is an option that can be turned off and on. If a database has been converted from an earlier version of Access, the option is turned off. Turn Name AutoCorrect on by choosing Tools⇔Options, clicking the General tab, and turning on the Track Name AutoCorrect Info and Perform Name AutoCorrect Options.

You can change the name of any object in a database using the same method you use to change the name of a Windows file in My Computer or Explorer:

1. In the Database window, click the name of the object once to select it.

2. Right-click to display the shortcut menu and choose Rename. Alternatively, you can click the object name a second time to edit it. (Note that this is not the same as double-clicking the object, which opens the object. A good way to ensure that you do not double-click is to move the mouse slightly between the two clicks.)

   Access displays the object name with a box around it.

3. Initially, the name is selected — you can type a new name to replace the current name. Or you can use a cursor control key (an arrow key) to display the cursor, and then edit the name.

4. Press Enter to accept the new name. (Press Esc if you decide not to change the name of the object after all.)

Deleting an object

When you delete an object, you delete the object definition. In the case of a table, you also delete the data stored in the table.

To delete an object, select it in the Database window and press Del. Access displays a warning, giving you the chance to change your mind. Click Yes to delete the object.

You cannot undo the deletion of a database object.

Copying objects

Occasionally, you may want to copy an object — perhaps you want to create a similar object, and copying and editing the original is more convenient than starting from scratch. Or maybe you want to create a backup before making significant changes. *See also* Part VIII for instructions.

Part III

Tables: A Home for Your Data

Tables are the basic building blocks of a database — they hold the raw data in the database. Forms, queries, and reports are all dependent on the data in the tables and the relationships between fields.

To create a useful database, you must first design your tables and fill them with data. This part contains all the information you need to know about tables and the data that goes in them — from creating a table with the Table Wizard to using a table to screen your data before you enter it into the database.

In this part . . .

- ✔ **Creating a table in Design view**
- ✔ **Creating a table in Datasheet view**
- ✔ **Creating a table with the Table Wizard**
- ✔ **Masking out incorrect data**
- ✔ **Entering data into a table**
- ✔ **Finding data in a table**
- ✔ **Defining and formatting fields**
- ✔ **Sorting and filtering tables**
- ✔ **Defining related fields to link tables in your database**

About Tables

Tables are the basic building block of your database — they store the data. One *table* stores a collection of related data in records and fields. *Fields* define each piece of information about an item, and these related fields are stored in *records*. Most databases have a number of tables. Each table stores a set of related data, and normally each table in the database is related to other tables through the repetition of a common field. *See also* Part I for an introduction to tables.

You can work with tables in two different views: Datasheet view and Design view.

Working in Datasheet view

A table in Datasheet view looks like a spreadsheet — it stores a collection of similar data in records and fields. *Records* store information for an item and appear as a row in the datasheet; *fields* define the type of information that is stored for each item and appear as columns in the datasheet.

The Datasheet view now enables you to see related records in other tables. A plus sign (+) appears to the left of records for which you can display related records from another table. *See also* "Displaying Related Records," in this part.

Display a list of tables by viewing the Database window and clicking the Tables button on the left side. To display a table in Datasheet view:

   ✦ Double-click the name of the table in the Database window.

   ✦ Select the table in the Database window and click the Open button on the toolbar.

 ✦ Click the Datasheet View button when the table is in Design view.

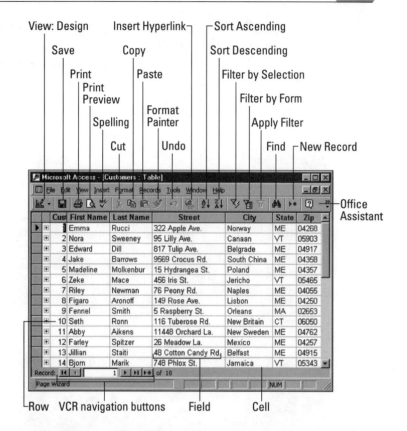

View: Design · Insert Hyperlink · Sort Ascending
Save · Copy · Sort Descending
Print · Paste · Filter by Selection
Print Preview · Filter by Form
Spelling · Format Painter · Apply Filter
Cut · Undo · Find · New Record

Cus	First Name	Last Name	Street	City	State	Zip
1	Emma	Rucci	322 Apple Ave.	Norway	ME	04268
2	Nora	Sweeney	95 Lilly Ave.	Canaan	VT	05903
3	Edward	Dill	817 Tulip Ave.	Belgrade	ME	04917
4	Jake	Barrows	9569 Crocus Rd.	South China	ME	04358
5	Madeline	Molkenbur	15 Hydrangea St.	Poland	ME	04357
6	Zeke	Mace	456 Iris St.	Jericho	VT	05465
7	Riley	Newman	76 Peony Rd.	Naples	ME	04055
8	Figaro	Aronoff	149 Rose Ave.	Lisbon	ME	04250
9	Fennel	Smith	5 Raspberry St.	Orleans	MA	02653
10	Seth	Ronn	116 Tuberose Rd.	New Britain	CT	06050
11	Abby	Aikens	11448 Orchard La.	New Sweden	ME	04762
12	Farley	Spitzer	26 Meadow La.	Mexico	ME	04257
13	Jillian	Staiti	48 Cotton Candy Rd.	Belfast	ME	04915
14	Bjorn	Marik	748 Phlox St.	Jamaica	VT	05343

Record: 1 of 18

Office Assistant

Row · VCR navigation buttons · Field · Cell

Working in Design view

Design view gives you ways to specify field properties and refine the table definition. You use Design view to define the type of data stored in a field, define the format of a field, identify the primary key, and enter data validation rules.

See also "Identifying Records with a Primary Key Field" and "Limiting Data Entries with a Validation Rule."

To display a table in Design view:

♦ Hold down the Ctrl key while you double-click the name of the table in the Database window.

♦ Select the table in the Database window and click the Design button on the toolbar.

♦ Right-click the table name in the Database window and choose Design from the shortcut menu.

♦ Click the Design View button when the table is in Datasheet view.

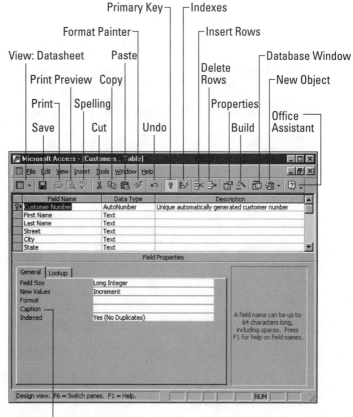

Field Properties

In Design view, each field gets a row, with the field name displayed in the first column, the type of data stored in the field displayed in the second column, and a description of the field displayed in the third column. The bottom half of the Design view window is called the Field Properties pane, and it displays additional options for the selected field (the one with a triangle in the row selector, immediately to the left of the field name). *See also* "Customizing Fields Using the Field Properties Pane," later in this part.

Adding a New Table to Your Database

You create a table by using the Table part of the Database window — three icons give you the following options:

- ✦ **Create Table in Design View:** Design the table in Design view by entering field names and data types, and perhaps using the more advanced Field Properties to define each field.

- ✦ **Create Table by Using Wizard:** Use a wizard to choose from commonly used table formats.

- ✦ **Create Table by Entering Data:** Create a new table by entering data and field names in a datasheet.

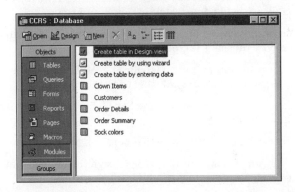

Alternatively, you can use the New Table dialog box. Open it by:

- ✦ Clicking the New button when the Table view is displayed in the Database window.

- ✦ Choosing Insert⇨Table from the menu when the database window is active.

- ✦ Opening the New Object button's drop-down list and choosing Table.

Creating a table in Datasheet view

Datasheet view is the most straightforward way to create a table. A datasheet looks like a spreadsheet — you can name your fields and begin entering data. Access figures out the type of data that each field holds. *See also* "Working in Datasheet view," in this part.

Creating a table in Datasheet view does not prevent you from using the more advanced settings in Design view. To display Design view at any time, click the Design View button.

Generally, tables hold only raw data, such as numbers, text, and dates. Calculations are reserved for queries, reports, and forms. Including calculations in tables dramatically and unnecessarily increases the size of the database.

Follow these steps to create a table in Datasheet view:

1. Display the Table view in the Database window and double-click the Create Table by Entering Data icon, or choose Datasheet View from the New Table dialog box.

Access creates a table called Table1. Across the top of the table are field names: Field1, Field2, and so on.

2. Enter one record of data (fill in the first row). Move to the next field by pressing Tab or Enter.

Access displays a pencil icon in the left border of the row to indicate that you are entering or changing data.

3. Save the table by clicking the Save button, pressing Ctrl+S, or choosing File⇨Save.

Access displays the Save As dialog box.

4. Type a new name for the table (assign the table a name that indicates what data is stored in it), and press Enter.

5. When Access asks whether you want to define a primary key, choose Yes or No. If you're not sure, choose No — you can go back to the table later to define a primary key, if you need to.

See also "Identifying Records with a Primary Key Field," later in this part.

When you save the table, Access gets rid of any additional columns in the datasheet. You can still add or remove fields, though. *See also* "Inserting a Column/Adding a Field" and "Deleting a Column/Removing a Field" for more information.

6. Rename a field by double-clicking the field name, typing a new name, and pressing Enter. Assign field names that reflect the data contained in them. Rename all the fields. Access automatically saves the new field names.

See also "Naming and Renaming Fields," later in this part.

7. Enter the rest of your data. Access automatically saves the data when you move to the next cell.

To move to the beginning of a row, press the Home key. To move to the next line when you've completed a record, press

Tab or Enter (this only works after you have saved the table the first time). You can also move to the next row by pressing the ↓ key.

See also "Adding Data to Your Database," later in this part.

 8. Close the table by clicking its Close button.

Creating a table in Design view

Design view is a good place to create your table if you want to use the more advanced settings, called *field properties,* available only in this view. Otherwise, Datasheet view usually works best.

You can only define fields in Design view — you can't enter any data. You have to use the Datasheet view or a form to do that.

To use Design view to create a table, follow these steps:

1. Click the Table button in the objects list of the Database window and double-click the Create Table in Design View icon or choose Design View from the New Table dialog box.

Access displays the Design view for the new, blank table called Table1. The cursor is in the first row, below the Field Name column heading.

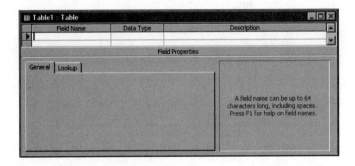

2. Type the name of the first field; then press Enter or Tab to move to the Data Type column.

Access displays the default Data Type, which is Text. As soon as you establish a data type for a field, Access displays field properties for that type of data in the Field Properties pane of the Design view window.

3. To view all data types, press F4 (or click the down arrow) to display the drop-down list of data type options.

4. Select the appropriate data type for the field.

See also "Changing Data Types," earlier in this part.

5. (Optional) Type a description in the third column (the one labeled Description).

The description you type appears in the status bar whenever the field is selected. Typing a description can give you and other users a hint about using the field.

6. Define additional fields in the table by repeating Steps 2 through 4.

7. Define a *primary key* (a field that uniquely identifies each record) by putting the cursor in the row with the primary key field and clicking the Primary Key button on the toolbar. Access displays a key to the left of the field name.

See also "Identifying Records with a Primary Key Field," later in this part.

8. Click the Save button or press Ctrl+S to display the Save As dialog box.

9. Type a new name for the table and then press Enter.

To enter data after you design the table, click the Datasheet View button to display Datasheet view. See also "About Tables" and "Adding Data to Your Database," in this part.

Creating a table using the Table Wizard

The Table Wizard simplifies the process of creating a table by allowing you to choose from among some common tables and often-used fields.

To create a table with the Table Wizard, follow these steps:

1. Begin the Table Wizard by:

   • Double-clicking the Create Table by Using Wizard icon in the Table view of the Database window.

   • Choosing Table Wizard from the New Table dialog box. (Display the New Table dialog box by clicking the New button in the Database window when the Table view is displayed.)

Access displays the first window of the Table Wizard.

2. If your database is for personal rather than business use, click the Personal radio button in the bottom-left corner to display tables and sample fields commonly used in personal applications.

3. Select a table in the Sample Tables list.

The field names in the Sample Fields list change to reflect the table you select. (Don't forget to use the scroll bars to see all the options.)

4. Add fields to the Fields in My New Table list by double-clicking the field name in the Sample Fields list. You can select all the fields in the Sample Fields list by clicking the double-right-arrow button.

The selected field(s) appears in the Fields in My New Table list.

5. If necessary, remove fields from the Fields in My New Table list.

To remove one field name, select it and click the left-arrow button to the left of the Fields in My New Table list. To remove all fields (maybe you need to start over!), click the double left-facing arrow that is beneath the left arrow button.

6. (Optional) You can rename a field by selecting it in the Fields in My New Table list and clicking the Rename Field button.

Access displays the Rename Field dialog box. Type the new name or edit the name displayed in the dialog box, and press Enter.

Any time after you select the table and fields, you can click Finish to accept the Table Wizard defaults and create the table.

7. Click Next to display the next Table Wizard window.

8. Change the name of the table (if you think it needs a better name) and use the radio buttons to tell Access whether you want it to set a primary key.

9. Click Next to display the next window. This window asks if any fields in the new table are related to any existing tables in the database.

10. If fields in the new table are related to fields in an existing table, select the table and click the Relationships button. Use the Relationships dialog box to tell Access how the tables are related; then click OK.

11. Click <u>N</u>ext to display the last window.

12. Click the radio button that describes what you want to do when the table is created.

13. Click <u>F</u>inish to create the table.

See also "Working with Wizards," in Part I.

Adding Data to Your Database

The easiest way to put data into a database, or to work with the data already there, is to use Datasheet view. Data can also be added to the database through forms and queries.

See also "About Tables," for a picture of the Datasheet view with all its various parts labeled. ***See also*** "Moving data from Excel," in Part VIII.

Here's how to add new records to an existing table:

1. Open the table in Datasheet view.

The easiest way to open a table is to double-click the table name in the Database window.

 2. Click the New Record button on the toolbar or at the bottom of the Datasheet.

Access moves the cursor to the last record, which is blank and waiting for input.

3. Type the appropriate information in the first field.

4. Press Enter or Tab after you type data in a cell to move to the next field. You can also click a cell to move the cursor to that cell.

5. Enter data in all the fields in the record (as needed) by repeating Steps 3 and 4. To enter data for another record, simply press Enter when the cursor is in the last field — Access automatically creates a new record.

 Access automatically saves the data in the database file when you move to the next record.

Blocking Unwanted Data with an Input Mask

An *input mask* limits the information allowed in a field by specifying what characters can be entered. An input mask is useful when you know the form the data should take — for instance, if an order number has two letters followed by four digits. Phone numbers and zip codes are other examples of fields where input masks are useful.

Another way to limit the information that can be entered in a field is to use a validation rule. Validation rules give you more flexibility in limiting the data that can be input. You can use an input mask with a validation rule to protect a field from data that is incorrect or that just doesn't belong there. ***See also*** "Limiting Data Entries with a Validation Rule," later in this part.

Input masks are commonly used in tables, but you can also add them to queries and forms where data may be entered. In all cases, you have to add an input mask from the Design view.

You can use an input mask to specify that the first character in a field must be a letter and every character after the first must be a number, for example. You can also use an input mask to add characters to a field — for example, use an input mask to display ten digits as a phone number, with parentheses around the first three digits and a dash after the sixth digit. If the data in a field varies or is not easily described, it's probably not a good candidate for an input mask.

The input mask for the field is in effect when data is being entered into the field in a datasheet or a form.

You can create input masks for text, number, and currency data; other data types don't have the Input Mask field property.

To create an input mask, enter a series of characters in the Input Mask section of the Field Properties pane to tell Access what kind of data to expect. Data that doesn't match the input mask cannot be entered. To block data from a field, first figure out exactly what data you want to allow in a field; then use the characters in the following table to code the data in the Input Mask field property in the table Design view. If you have trouble formulating an input mask, you may find that a validation rule meets your needs better.

Input Mask Character	What It Allows/Requires
0	Requires a number; + and - not allowed
9	Allows a number; + and - not allowed
#	Allows a space, converts a blank to a space, allows + and -

(continued)

Input Mask Character	What It Allows/Requires
L	Requires a letter
?	Allows a letter
A	Requires a letter or number
a	Allows a letter or number
C	Allows any character or a space
<	Converts the following characters to lowercase
>	Converts the following characters to uppercase
!	Fills field from right to left, allowing characters on the left side to be optional
\	Displays the character following in the field (\Z appears as Z)
. ,	Displays the decimal placeholder or thousands separator
; : - /	Displays the date separator (the symbol used depends on the setting in the Regional Settings section of the Windows Control Panel)

The Input Mask Wizard can help you enter the input mask for your data — especially if the data in the field is a common type of data, such as a phone number or a zip code. And if your data is similar to one of the data types in the Input Mask Wizard you may want to use the wizard and then edit the input mask in Design view.

To use the Input Mask Wizard, follow these steps:

1. Display the table in Design view.

2. Select the field you want to apply an Input Mask to.

3. Click Input Mask in the Field Properties pane of the window.

 4. Click the Build button that appears to the right of the property.

Access displays the Input Mask Wizard (it may take a while).

5. Select the input mask that looks like the data that you want to allow in the field.

6. Click the Try It box.

Access displays the field as it looks before data is entered — blank spaces are shown as underscores, and any punctuation, like hyphens or parentheses, is displayed.

7. Type some text to see how the field appears with data in it.

8. Click <u>N</u>ext to see more questions about the input mask. The questions you see depend on the type of data you chose in the first window. Access displays a Try It box on the window so that you can see the effect of any changes you make — click in the Try It box to see what the input mask looks like when data is being entered in the field.

Click Finish to accept the default settings and skip additional wizard windows.

9. If necessary, click Next to display the final window of the wizard.

10. Click Finish to tell the wizard to put the input mask it helped you create into the Input Mask property for the field.

Access displays the Design view with the new Input Mask.

11. Save the table design by clicking the Save button — otherwise, you may lose your nifty new input mask!

You can add an input mask to the list displayed in the wizard by clicking the Edit List button on the first window of the Input Mask Wizard and filling in the details of the new input mask.

Changing Column Width

Initially, Access gives all columns in a datasheet the same width. You can change the width one column at a time, or a few columns at once.

To change the width of one column, follow these steps:

1. Move the mouse pointer to the right border of the column and then up to the top of the column, where the field names appear.

The pointer turns into the change-column-width pointer.

2. Click and drag the column border to a new position.

You can change the width of several adjacent columns at the same time using this method — simply select all the columns (click the first column header and drag to the header for the last column that you want to select). Change the width of one of the selected columns. All the selected columns become the same width as the one column whose width you changed.

You can also tell Access to change the column width so that the column is wide enough for the widest data in the column. To size the column to fit the contents, move the mouse pointer so that you see the change-column-width pointer, and double-click.

Changing Data Types

Fields need to have a *type*, which describes the kind of data that can be entered into the field. Common data types are text, numeric, and date/time. The following table describes each data type:

Data Type	What It Holds
Text	The Text type can contain numbers, letters, punctuation, spaces, and special characters (such as #, @, !, and %). If you use hyphens or parentheses in phone numbers (and almost everyone does), the phone-number field is defined as a text field. You can't use a number in a text field in calculations (but who wants to add phone numbers?). A text field holds up to 255 characters.
Memo	The Memo type can contain numbers, letters, spaces, and special characters, just like the Text type, but more of them fit in a Memo field than in a Text field — up to 65,535 characters. (You really have to work to fill up this type of field!)
Number	The Number type can contain only numbers. You may use + and – before the number, and a decimal point as long as it is followed by at least one number. You can use Number fields in calculations.
Date/Time	The Date/Time type can hold, well, dates and times. You can do calculations with Date/Time fields.
Currency	The Currency type holds numbers with a currency sign in front of them ($, £, ¥, and so on). You can do calculations with Currency fields. (A font with the new Euro symbol is available from the Microsoft Web site.)
AutoNumber	The AutoNumber type includes numbers unique to each record. Access assigns these numbers starting at 1, and automatically increments subsequent records.
Yes/No	The Yes/No type holds any kind of yes-or-no data. You can set up a Yes/No field to contain other two-word sets, such as True/False, On/Off, and Male/Female, and so on.
OLE Object	The OLE Object type can hold a picture, a sound, or another object created with OLE-compatible software other than Access.
Hyperlink	The Hyperlink type can hold links to World Wide Web addresses (URLs), objects within the database, files, and other kinds of hyperlink addresses.
Lookup Wizard	The Lookup Wizard type runs the Lookup Wizard, which enables you to select a table or type a list to display in a drop-down list used for data entry. **See also** "Creating a Lookup Field," in this part.

If you create your table in Datasheet view and enter data, Access selects a data type based on the entered data. If you enter text,

Access makes the data type of the field Text. If you enter numbers with a currency symbol in front, Access sets the data type to Currency.

To change the data type Access chooses, use the Data Type setting for the field in Design view. Follow these steps:

1. Switch to Design view by clicking the Design View button.

2. Click the Data Type column of the field whose data type you want to change.

3. Display the drop-down list by clicking the down-arrow key or by pressing F4.

4. Choose the data type that you want by clicking it.

You can also cycle through the data types without displaying the drop-down list by double-clicking the Data Type setting.

Changing Row Height

You can change row heights in the same way that you change column widths. Changing row height has a catch, though — when you change the height of one row, the heights of all the other rows in the datasheet change, too. You can wrap text on a datasheet by making the row tall enough to fit multiple lines.

	First Name	Last Name	Street	City	State	Zi
Zac	Young	322 Apple Ave.	Norway	ME	0426
Tyler	Sweeney	95 Lilly Ave.	Canaan	VT	0590
Edward	Dill	817 Tulip Ave.	Belgrade	ME	0491
Jake	Barrows	9569 Crocus Rd.	South China	ME	0435
Madeline	Molkenbur	15 Hydrangea St.	Poland	ME	0435
Zeke	Mace	456 Iris St.	Jericho	VT	0546
Riley	Newman	76 Peony Rd.	Naples	ME	0405

Customers : Table

Record: 1 of 16

Change the height of rows in a datasheet by using one of these methods:

◆ Click and drag between rows in the row selector boxes. (To make a row exactly two lines tall, use the row borders as a guide as you drag the change-row-height pointer.)

✛　✦ Use the Row Height dialog box. Display it by right-clicking a row selector and choosing <u>R</u>ow Height.

Copying a Field

You can copy a field. This capability is particularly useful if you are creating several similar fields — rather than defining the data type and properties for each field, you can simply copy a field definition and edit the field as necessary.

You may want to copy a field that you are using to link tables. This ensures that the field has the same properties in both tables, a requirement for related fields.

Follow these steps to copy a field:

1. Display the table in Design view.

2. Select the field you want to copy by clicking the row selector.

3. Copy the field by clicking the Copy button or choosing <u>E</u>dit⇨<u>C</u>opy.

4. Move to a blank row or create a blank row by right-clicking within a row and choosing Insert Rows from the shortcut menu. If you're copying the field to a different table, display that table in Design view and move to a blank row.

5. Click the Paste button or choose <u>E</u>dit⇨<u>P</u>aste.

Notice that Access copies the field properties as well as the information in the selected row.

6. Type a new name to rename the copied field.

Access has the field name selected, so typing a new name replaces the selected name.

7. Press Enter to complete the new field.

8. Edit the Description, if necessary.

9. Save the table.

You can copy the field again by moving to another blank row and clicking the Paste button.

Creating a Lookup Field

You can create your own drop-down list in a table to guide others (or yourself) as they enter data. A lookup field provides the user with a list of choices, rather than requiring users to type a value into the datasheet. Lookup fields enable you to keep your database small and the data entered in it accurate and consistent.

The items on the drop-down list can come from a list you type, or from a field in another table. For example, you may want to input the customer number when you know the customer name. Using the Lookup Wizard, you can tell Access to display a drop-down list in the Customer Number field that displays the first and last name as well as the customer number. When a customer is selected, the customer number is put in the table. (It's not as confusing as it sounds. Trust me.)

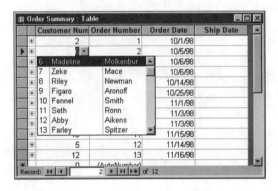

Access has a Lookup Wizard to help you create lookup fields. Here's how to use it:

1. Display the table in Design view.

2. Display the drop-down list for the Data Type for the field that will contain the drop-down list and select Lookup Wizard.

3. Tell the wizard whether the values you want to appear on the field's drop-down list are coming from a field in another table or from a list that you type.

If the field simply consists of several choices, choose the second option and type the list. But if you want to store more information about those choices (maybe you're entering the name of a customer who bought something, but you also want to store the customer's address and phone number in another table), store the values in a table.

If you don't want the drop-down list to display every value in the field in another table, you can base the drop-down list on a field in a query. *See also* "Adding a Select Query to the Database," in Part IV.

4. Click <u>N</u>ext to display the next window of the Lookup Wizard.

What you see in the second window depends on the option you choose in the first window:

- If you ask the lookup field to display values from another table, Access asks you about the name of the table.

- If you tell Access that you want to type in the values, you get a table in which you can type the lookup list.

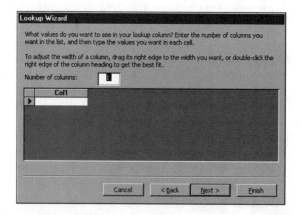

5. If you're typing values to choose among, click in the table in the wizard window (which currently has only one cell), and type the first entry in the list. Press Tab — not Enter — to create new cells for additional entries.

If you want your lookup list to include values stored in a table or query, select the object containing the field with the values you want to choose among. You can choose an existing query by clicking the Queries or Both radio button.

6. Click <u>N</u>ext to display the next window.

7. If you typed a list, this screen you see is the last screen of the wizard — skip to Step 12. If you're using a table for the lookup, you have to tell Access which field(s) you want to use by moving field names from the Available Fields list box to the Selected Fields list box.

See also Part I, for more information on choosing fields in windows such as this one.

If you pick multiple fields, the information in each field is displayed on the drop-down list. However, only one field's information can be stored, so the next window asks you which field's value you want to store in the new field. For instance, you may display the Customer Number, First Name, and Last Name in the drop-down list, but you can only store one of those values — in the example in the figure, that value is the Customer Number.

8. Click Next to display the next window.

This window shows you a table with the values in the lookup list, and allows you to change the width of the columns. The window also contains a check box which, when selected, hides the key field (if you selected the key field). Depending on your application, you may want to display the key field by unselecting the Hide Key Column check box. **See also** "Identifying Records with a Primary Key Field."

9. Change the width of the column if necessary.

You can change the width of the column to automatically fit the widest entry by double-clicking the right edge of the field name that appears at the top of the column.

See also "Changing Column Width," earlier in this part.

10. Click Next to display the final window of this wizard.

11. Edit the name that Access gives the lookup column, if you want, and then click Finish to create the lookup column.

12. Now check out your lookup list by viewing your table in Datasheet view. When you click the field for which you created the lookup list, you see an arrow that indicates that a drop-down list is available. Click the arrow to see options in the list.

The default setting lets users either choose from the drop-down list or type in a value. To force users to choose from the drop-down list (or enter a value that is on the drop-down list), click the Lookup tab in the Field Properties pane and change the Limit To List setting from No to Yes.

You can add values to an existing lookup list. If you typed values for the lookup list yourself, switch to Design view, click the field with the lookup, and click the Lookup tab in the Field Properties pane. You can add options to the Row Source — separate the values with a semicolon. If the lookup list gets its values from a table, you can add records to the table to see additional choices in the lookup list.

The lookup field is not automatically updated when you add additional items. Refresh the data in the lookup field by pressing F9.

Lookups can be more complex than I have the space to cover here. The Access Help system provides extensive information on Lookup fields.

 For more information about lookups, check out *Access 2000 Bible* (IDG Books Worldwide, Inc.).

Customizing Fields Using the Field Properties Pane

Field properties (which appear at the bottom of a window in Design view) enable you to format a field and disallow certain entries. The part of the Design view that contains the field properties is called the *Field Properties pane* (a pane being part of a window — cute, eh?). The properties you see in this pane depend on the data type you choose. Although many properties appear for all data types, not all properties appear for all data types.

To change a field property, you have to tell Access which field you're working with. Display your table in Design view and click somewhere in the row that contains the field you want to work with. You can also click the row selector — the gray box to the left of the field name. (The field you're currently working with has an arrow in the row selector.)

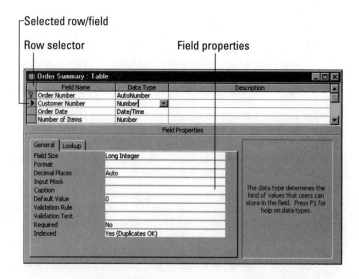

The field properties shown in the preceding figure are for a Number field. The properties you see vary depending on the type of field that's active.

Access can help you format field properties. Click a property; if you see an arrow to the right of the property, Access has pre-defined settings for that property. If you see a Build button to the right of the property, click that button to display a dialog box or wizard that helps fill in the property for you.

See also "Blocking Unwanted Data with an Input Mask," "Limiting Data Entries with a Validation Rule," "Formatting Fields," and "Setting Field Size," all in this part, for information about using field properties.

Deleting a Column/Removing a Field

 You can delete a field from a table, but you should do so very carefully — a 24-hour waiting period may be in order. When you delete a field (a column in a datasheet), you also irretrievably delete all the data in the field.

To delete a field in Datasheet view, follow these steps:

1. Right-click the field name for the column.

Access selects the column and displays the shortcut menu.

2. Choose Delete Column from the shortcut menu.

Access displays a warning box, telling you that you will permanently delete the field and the data in it.

3. Click Yes to delete the field (or No if you change your mind).

To delete a field in Design view, follow the same procedure, except right-click the row selector for the field that you want to delete and choose Delete Rows from the shortcut menu.

Deleting Records

To delete a record in a datasheet, follow these steps:

1. Right-click the row selector of the record that you want to delete.

2. Choose Delete Record from the shortcut menu.

 Alternatively, you can put the cursor anywhere in the row that you want to delete and then click the Delete Record button.

 Deleting a record is permanent. When you delete data, you can't get it back — so make sure that you really want to delete it!

Displaying Related Records

A new feature in Access 2000 allows you to display related records from another table in a *subdatasheet*. If subdatasheets are available, you will see a + at the beginning of the record. Click the + to see the subdatasheet.

	Cus	First Name	Last Name	Street	City	State
⊞	7	Zeke	Mace	456 Iris St.	Jericho	VT
⊞	8	Riley	Newman	76 Peony Rd.	Naples	ME
⊟	9	Figaro	Aronoff	149 Rose Ave.	Lisbon	ME

Customers : Table

	Order Number	Order Date	Ship Date
⊞	9	11/3/98	11/5/98
*	(AutoNumber)		

	Cus	First Name	Last Name	Street	City	State
⊞	10	Fennel	Smith	5 Raspberry St.	Orleans	MA
⊞	11	Seth	Ronn	116 Tuberose Rd.	New Britain	CT
⊞	12	Abby	Aikens	11448 Orchard La.	New Sweden	ME
⊞	13	Farley	Spitzer	26 Meadow La.	Mexico	ME
⊞	14	Jillian	Staiti	48 Cotton Candy Rd.	Belfast	ME
⊞	15	Bjorn	Marik	748 Phlox St.	Jamaica	VT
⊞	16	Cally	Vincens-Cook	78442 Delphinium Ave.	Berlin	CT
⊞	17	Edgar	Patterson	89 Rhododendron Rd.	Berlin	MA

Record: 1 of 1

Access automatically creates subdatasheets in a datasheet if it has a one-to-one relationship with another table, or if it is on the one side of a one-to-many relationship with another table. You may use subdatasheets in query datasheets also.

You can display and hide subdatasheets using the following techniques:

◆ Click + to display the subdatasheet for one record.

◆ Click - to hide the displayed subdatasheet.

◆ Choose Format➪Subdatasheet➪Expand All to display all subdatasheets on the datasheet.

◆ Choose Format➪Subdatasheet➪Collapse All to hide all subdatasheets on the datasheet.

◆ Choose Format➪Subdatasheet➪Remove to remove subdatasheets from the datasheet. To reverse this step you must change the table properties as described below.

When a subdatasheet is displayed, you can use it as you would the table that holds the data. The most useful way to use a subdatasheet is to enter data into it — just use the New Record button in the subdatasheet to create a new record, then enter data as you normally do.

Access determines which table to display as a subdatasheet based on the relationships you have defined in the database. However, you can select a table or query to be used as a subdatasheet by following these steps:

1. Select Insert⇨Subdatasheet from the menu to see the Insert Subdatasheet dialog box.

2. Select the table you want to use as a subdatasheet. If you want to use a query for the subdatasheet, click the Queries tab and select the query you want to use.

3. In the Link Child Fields option, select the field you want to use to link to in the query or table you've chosen as the subdatasheet.

4. In the Link Master Fields option, select the field you want to use to link from in the original table — the one displayed when you started Step 1. The two link fields will probably be fields that you have defined as related. At the very least, they will contain similar information (like a customer number).

5. Click OK to close the dialog box.

You can edit the subdatasheet by repeating the steps. You can also control subdatasheets from the Table Properties — the last four properties control subdatasheets. (Display table properties by right-clicking the table Design view and selecting Properties.)

Subdatasheets in tables and queries are not available in Access Projects.

Editing Data in a Datasheet

Edit a value by moving the cursor to the value, pressing F2, or clicking on the value to see a cursor. Delete characters by using the Delete and Backspace keys. Add new characters by typing them.

To replace the contents of a field, select the entire field by clicking at the beginning of the field, holding the mouse button down, and dragging the mouse pointer to the end of the field. Then type the new entry — whatever you type replaces the selected characters.

See also "Moving Around in a Datasheet," later in this part.

Filtering Your Data

Filtering allows you to look at a subset of your table — records that match a particular criteria. (In English, this means that you can create a test for your data to pass, and then look only at the rows in your table that pass your test.) In Access, a criterion for filtering is something like "I want to find all the records with 2 in the Number of Items field." To use more advanced criteria such as "2 or more" or "between 3 and 20," you need to use the Advanced Filter/Sort command or a query. *See also* "Sorting a Query," in Part IV and "Creating a Report from a Filtered Table," in Part V.

When filtering doesn't give you the options you need, you probably need to use a query. *See also* "About Queries," in Part IV.

You can filter in three ways: Filter by Selection, Filter by Form, and Advanced Filter/Sort. The following table explains when you need to use each filtering option:

Type of Filter	When You Need to Use It
Filter by Selection	When you have only one criterion for one field that filtered records need to meet, and you can find one record that matches your criterion.
Filter by Form	When you have more than one criterion to match. For instance, if you are looking for orders over $50 that were sent before December 1.
Advanced Filter/Sort	When you have more complex criteria than can be defined in a Filter by Form. Choosing Advanced Filter/Sort creates a query. Use this option when what you really want is to create a query that uses only one table.

Filtering creates a temporary table containing only those records that fit the criteria you choose. If you want a permanent table that updates as more records are added, you need to create a query. *See also* "Creating a Query," in Part IV.

You can tell when a table is filtered by looking at the bottom of the table — the status bar tells you how many records are in the table and displays "Filtered" in parentheses.

You can't save a filter — if you want to be able to use a filtered table later, you need to create a query that contains the same criterion as your filter.

Filtering by selection

To filter by selection, you first need to find a record that matches your criterion. To find all the Maine addresses in your address table, for example, you need to find an address that has ME in the State field.

Follow these steps to filter a table by selection:

1. Put the cursor in the record and field that matches the criterion.

To find all addresses in Maine, for example, you may put the cursor in the State field that contains the abbreviation ME.

2. Click the Filter by Selection button or choose Records⇨ Filter⇨Filter by Selection.

Access creates a temporary table consisting of the records that meet the criterion. Access finds records that have identical entries in the selected field.

	First Name	Last Name	Street	City	State	Zip
▶	Zac	Young	322 Apple Ave.	Norway	ME	04268
	Edward	Dill	817 Tulip Ave.	Belgrade	ME	04917
	Jake	Barrows	9569 Crocus Rd.	South China	ME	04358
	Madeline	Molkenbur	15 Hydrangea St.	Poland	ME	04358
	Riley	Newman	76 Peony Rd.	Naples	ME	04055
	Figaro	Aronoff	149 Rose Ave.	Lisbon	ME	04250
	Abby	Aikens	11448 Orchard La.	New Sweden	ME	04762
	Farley	Spitzer	26 Meadow La.	Mexico	ME	04257
	Flash	Staiti	48 Cotton Candy Rd.	Belfast	ME	04915
*						

Record: 14 ◄ 1 ► ►I ►* of 9 (Filtered)

If you haven't narrowed the list down enough, you can filter the filtered table again by using the same technique. You can choose a different field, or even select just one word or part of a field, before clicking the Filter by Selection button.

To see the entire table again, click the Remove Filter button.

You can select particular records that you want to filter out and then choose Records⇨Filter⇨Filter Excluding Selection to exclude the selected records from the table. Use this technique in combination with the Filter by Selection command to see only the records you want to see. To see the entire table, click the Apply Filter button again.

Filtering by form

If you have more than one criterion, filter by form. The Filter by Form window enables you to pick the values you want the filtered records to have. Unlike the Filter by Selection command, however, Filter by Form allows you to choose more than one value and to choose values to match for more than one field.

When you filter by form, you can use multiple criteria. If you specify more than one criterion on a Filter by Form tab, Access treats the criteria as AND criteria, meaning that a record has to pass *all* the criteria in order to be displayed on the filtered datasheet.

If you use criteria on different tabs (using the OR tab at the bottom of the window to display a clean grid), Access treats the criteria as OR criteria. That means that a record has to meet the criteria on one tab or the other to be included on the filtered datasheet.

Using AND and OR criteria enables you to filter the records using more than one rule or set of rules. For example, you can find addresses from South China, ME, as well as addresses in Vermont by using the OR tab at the bottom of the Filter by Form window.

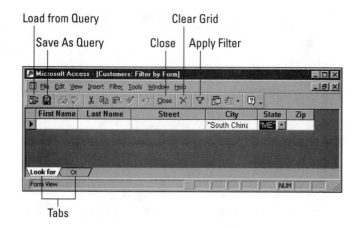

Tabs

Follow these steps to filter a datasheet by form:

1. Click the Filter by Form button or choose Records⇨Filter⇨ Filter by Form.

Access displays the Filter by Form window, which looks like an empty datasheet with some different buttons in the toolbar and some different menu choices.

2. Move the cursor to a field you have a criterion for.

A down arrow appears in the field the cursor is in.

3. Click the arrow to see the list of all the values for that field.

4. Click the value that you want the filtered records to match.

If you want the criterion to specify part of the value in the field, type **LIKE "*value that you're looking for*"**. For example, typing **LIKE "n"** in the Name field finds all records in the Name field containing the letter *n*.

5. If you have criteria for another field that should be applied at the same time as the criterion you set in Step 4 (AND criteria), repeat Steps 3 and 4 for the additional field.

For example, if you want to find addresses in San Francisco, CA, set the State field to CA and the City field to San Francisco.

6. If you have another set of rules to filter records by, click the Or tab at the bottom of the Filter by Form window.

Access displays a blank Filter by Form window. When you set criteria on more than one tab, a record only has to meet all the criteria on any one tab to be displayed on the filtered datasheet.

7. Choose the criteria on the second tab in the same way that you chose those on the first — click the field, and choose the value that you want to match.

For example, if, in addition to all the addresses in San Francisco, you want to see all addresses from Boston, MA, set the State field on the new Filter by Form grid to MA and the City field to Boston.

Another Or tab appears, allowing you to continue adding as many sets of OR criteria as you need.

 8. To see the filtered table, click the Apply Filter button.

You have a few more options when you use the Filter by Form window:

If You Want to . . .	*Here's How to Do It*
Delete a tab's worth of criteria	Click the tab and then choose Edit⇨Delete Tab.
Delete all criteria	Click the Clear Grid button.
Save the filter as a query, so that you can see it later	Click the Save As Query button, give the new query a name, and click the OK button. To see the query, click the Queries tab of the Database window.
See the entire table	Click the Apply Filter button.
See the filtered table again	Click the Apply Filter button.
Use an expression as a criterion	Type the expression in the field to which it applies. *See also* "Limiting Records with Criteria Expressions," in Part IV.

Finding Data in a Table

To find a record that contains a particular word or value, use the Find and Replace dialog box.

To display the Find and Replace dialog box, open a datasheet and do one of the following:

✦ Press Ctrl+F.

✦ Choose Edit⇨Find.

 ✦ Click the Find button.

To use the Find and Replace dialog box, follow these steps:

1. In Datasheet view, put the cursor in the field that contains the value you're searching for.

2. Display the Find and Replace dialog box.

3. In the Find What box, type the text or value that you're looking for.

4. Use the Look In option to determine where to look — in the field your cursor is in, or in the whole table.

5. Use the Match option to determine whether you're looking for part of a field (Any Part of Field); you want an exact match for the whole field (Whole Field); or if you want the field to start with the text in the Find What box (Start of Field).

6. Click Find Next to find the first instance of the value or text in the table.

Access displays the section of the table containing the values in the Find What box.

7. If you do not find what you're looking for, click Find Next until you do.

 You can display more options on the Find and Replace dialog box by clicking the More button. Use the settings in the Find and Replace dialog box to find exactly what you're looking for:

✦ **Search:** This option determines the direction in which Access searches. Choose Up, Down, or All. Choose All to find the text or value anywhere in the table — however, Access starts the search at the cursor.

✦ **Match:** Choose Any Part of Field, Whole Field, or Start of Field to tell Access whether the value or text that you typed is in the entire field, at the beginning of the field, or anywhere in the field (which means that the text may start somewhere in the middle of the field).

✦ **Match Case:** When you activate this check box, Access finds only text that matches the case of the text that you type in the Find What box.

✦ **Search Fields As Formatted:** This option matches the contents of the Find What box to the formatted data (the way the data appears in the table, using the format and input mask properties, rather than the way it was entered). *See also* "Customizing Fields Using the Field Properties Pane," earlier in this part.

✦ **Replace With:** Use this option on the Replace tab of the Find and Replace dialog box to replace instances of the Find What text with the Replace With text. Replace one instance at a time by clicking the Replace button. Replace all instances by clicking the Replace All button.

Formatting Datasheets

Although you don't have the flexibility in formatting datasheets that you do with reports and forms, you do have some options. You can change the font, row height, column width, and some other options. To change a datasheet's format, use the Format menu. (A datasheet has to be the active window for you to see this menu.)

Changing the font

You can change the font and font size in your datasheet by using the Font dialog box. You cannot change the font of just one cell, column or row — changing the font changes the whole datasheet. Display the Font dialog box by choosing Format➪Font.

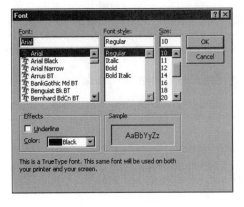

Displaying and removing gridlines

Gridlines are the gray horizontal and vertical lines that separate cells in a datasheet. You can change the color of the gridlines displayed in a datasheet or not display gridlines at all. You can also give cells some special effects, rather than simply separating them with gridlines.

To change gridlines, choose <u>F</u>ormat⇨Datasheet. Access displays the Datasheet Formatting dialog box.

As you change the settings, the Sample box shows the effect of the changes on the datasheet.

Here's what the options on the Datasheet Formatting dialog box do to your datasheet:

Option	What It Does
Horizontal	Displays or hides horizontal gridlines
Vertical	Displays or hides vertical gridlines
Cell Effect: Flat, Raised, or Sunken	Displays the cells normally (Flat) or with a three-dimensional effect
Background Color	Allows you to choose a background color for cells
Gridline Color	Allows you to choose a gridline color
Border and Line Styles	Allows you to change the look of the border, horizontal gridline, vertical gridline, and column header underline. Select the line that you want to format in the first box, and choose the line style in the second box.

Formatting Fields

When you're working with a table in Design view, you can format various fields by using the Format setting in the Field Properties pane. These options change how the data appears in the table, and may affect how the data appears in queries, forms, and reports.

Formatting Text and Memo fields

When you're dealing with a Text field, the Format options of the Field Properties pane enable you to specify how the text in a field should appear, as well as how many characters may be entered in the field.

To format Text and Memo fields, type the characters in the following table into the Format section of the Field Properties pane:

Formatting for Text	*What You Type*
Display text all uppercase	>
Display text all lowercase	<
Display text left-aligned	!
Specify a color	[*color*] (black, blue, green, cyan, magenta, yellow, and white are the color options)
Specify a certain number of characters	@ (Type @ for each character to be included — including spaces)
Specify that no character is required	&
Display text	**/text**

You can tell Access to add characters such as +, —, $, a comma, parentheses, or a space to the data entered. For example, you may want to enter the following in the Format setting for a phone number:

(@@@) @@@ - @@@@

If you then enter ten digits into this field, the numbers appear with parentheses and the hyphen, even though you don't type those extra characters.

You can even format fields to include additional text. Just enclose the text you want to add in quotation marks or precede it with a slash (/).

You can use the input mask option to help you with formatting. The input mask controls text as it is entered — format options affect how the data is displayed. *See also* "Blocking Unwanted Data with an Input Mask," earlier in this part.

Formatting Number and Currency fields

Access has common formats for Number and Currency fields built right in — all you have to do is choose the format that you want from the Format drop-down list in the Field Properties pane.

General Number	3456.789
Currency	$3,456.79
Fixed	3456.79
Standard	3,456.79
Percent	123.00%
Scientific	3.46E+03

The following tables describe the different formats from which you can choose:

Number Format	How It Works
Number	Displays numbers without commas and with as many decimal places as the user enters
Currency	Displays numbers with the local currency symbol (determined from the Regional Settings found in the Windows Control Panel), commas as thousands separators, and two decimal places
Fixed	Displays numbers with the number of decimal places specified in the Decimal Places setting (immediately below the Format setting); the default is 2
Standard	Displays numbers with commas as thousands separators and the number of decimal places specified in the Decimal Places property
Percent	Displays numbers as percentages — that is, multiplied by 100 and followed by a percent sign
Scientific	Displays numbers in scientific notation

If the numbers in the field don't seem to be formatted according to the Number Format property, you may need to change the Field Size property. For example, if you have the Field Size property set to Integer or Long Integer, it doesn't matter what value you use in the Decimal Places property, Access insists on displaying the value as an integer — with no decimal places. Try using Single or Double in the Format property instead.

You can define your own number format by using the following symbols in the Format field property instead of choosing from the drop-down list:

Symbol	What It Does
#	Displays a value if one is input for that place
0	Displays a 0 if no value appears in that place; otherwise, displays the input value
.	Displays a decimal point
,	Displays a comma
$ (or other currency symbol)	Displays a currency symbol
%	Displays the number in percent format
E+00	Displays scientific notation

You can, for example, create a number format with comma separators and three decimal places by typing the following in the Format property:

###,##0.000

Formatting Date/Time fields

Access has built-in Date/Time formats from which you can choose. To see these formats, display the drop-down list in the Format section of the Field Properties pane.

Next to each format name is an example of how the date and/or time is displayed. If you don't specify a format for a Date/Time field, Access uses the General Date format.

General Date	6/19/94 5:34:23 PM
Long Date	Sunday, June 19, 1994
Medium Date	19-Jun-94
Short Date	6/19/94
Long Time	5:34:23 PM
Medium Time	5:34 PM
Short Time	17:34

You can create your own Date/Time format if you don't like the ones that Access offers on the drop-down list. To see what characters you can use to create your own Date/Time format, do the following:

1. Select a Date/Time field in Table Design view.

2. Move your cursor to the Format field property — the first option in the Field Properties pane at the bottom of the window.

3. Press F1.

Access displays general help on the Format property.

To see help specific to creating your own Date/Time format, click the Date/Time Data Type link.

Freezing a Column in a Datasheet

When you're working with a wide datasheet, you may want to freeze one column so that you can move all the way to the right edge of the table and still see that particular field. When you freeze a column, it moves to the left side of the window (no matter where it appeared before) and stays there, even when you scroll or pan all the way to the right.

To freeze a column, follow these steps:

1. Right-click the field name to select the column and display the shortcut menu.

2. Select Freeze Columns to freeze the selected column.

You can select more than one consecutive column to freeze by clicking the first field name and dragging to the last one, but then you have to choose Format⇨Freeze Columns from the menu to freeze the columns. You can't display the shortcut menu without deselecting all but one of the columns.

To unfreeze a column, choose Format⇨Unfreeze All Columns.

The freeze and unfreeze column commands may be hidden the first time you display the Format menu.

Identifying Records with a Primary Key Field

A *primary key* uniquely identifies every record in a table. Most of the time, the primary key is a single field, but it can also be a combination of fields, in which case it is called a *multiple-field primary key.* Examples of a primary key field are Social Security Number, a unique customer number, or some other field that uniquely identifies the record.

You can identify an existing field as the primary key, or you can ask Access to create one. To have Access create a primary key for you, follow these steps:

1. Close the table.

Access asks whether you want to create a primary key.

2. Select Yes.

Access creates a field called ID in the first column of the table. The field starts at 1 and increases by 1 for each record (it's an AutoNumber field). Access automatically inserts a new number each time you add a new record to the table.

You can also create a primary key in Design view. Click the cursor in the field you want to make the primary key and click the Primary Key button. Access displays the key symbol to the left of the field name.

To make an autonumber primary key field, create an autonumber field and designate it as the primary key.

To make a *multiple-field primary key,* select the fields in Design view. To select a field, click the row selector — the gray block to the left of the field name. Then Ctrl+click to select fields after you select the first field. When the fields are selected, click the Primary Key button.

Inserting a Column/Adding a Field

Inserting a column into a datasheet gives you the space to add a new field to the table. You can add a field to your table using either Datasheet or Design view.

To add a column in Datasheet view, follow these steps:

1. Right-click the field name of the column to the right of where you want the new column.

Access selects the column and displays the shortcut menu.

2. Choose Insert Column from the shortcut menu.

To add a field in Design view, follow these steps:

1. Right-click the row selector of the field that will immediately follow the field you're inserting.

Access selects the row and displays the shortcut menu.

2. Choose Insert Rows from the shortcut menu.

Access adds a row. Now you can define your field.

Limiting Data Entries with a Validation Rule

Often, you know exactly what kind of data you want people to type in to a certain field. The *Validation Rule* field property (in the Field Properties pane) enables you to specify a rule that data must pass in order to be entered in a particular field.

If someone using your database attempts to enter data that does not pass your validation rule, the contents of the Validation Text field property pop up to guide the user.

To create a validation rule, follow these steps:

1. Display the table in Design view.

2. Select the field to which you want to add a validation rule.

3. Click Validation Rule in the General tab of the Field Properties pane.

4. Enter your validation rule. The following information tells you how to create your validation rule.

5. Enter the validation text. This text appears when data that does not meet the validation rule is entered.

Use operators to tell Access how to validate your data. *Operators* are symbols like < and > and words like AND and NOT that you use to tell Access how to limit your data. (+, —, *, and / are also operators, but you aren't as likely to use them in validation rules.)

Validation Rule Example	How It Works
"Boston" OR "New York"	Limits input in the field to just those two cities.
Is Null	The user is allowed to leave the field blank.
<10	Only values less than 10 are allowed.
>10	Only values greater than 10 are allowed.
<=10	Only values less than or equal to 10 are allowed.
>=10	Only values greater than or equal to 10 are allowed.
=10	Only values equal to 10 are allowed.
<>0	Only values not equal to 0 are allowed.
IN("Boston", "Concord")	Only text that is *Boston* or *Concord* is allowed.
BETWEEN 10 AND 20	Only values between 10 and 20 are allowed.

The LIKE operator deserves its own explanation. Use the LIKE operator to test whether an input matches a certain pattern — use wildcard characters to help define the pattern.

Wildcard	What It Signifies
?	Any single character
#	Any single number
*	Zero or more characters

For example, you may define a zip code field to only allow five digits, as follows:

```
LIKE "#####"
```

You can also define a field to contain only names that start with the letter S, as follows:

```
LIKE "S*"
```

According to the preceding rule, a person can choose not to type any characters after the S, because the * allows zero or more characters. If you want the S to always be followed a certain number of characters, use the ? wildcard, instead. For example, if you want people to type exactly three characters after the letter S, use this validation rule:

```
LIKE "S???"
```

You can use more than one expression in a validation rule by separating the expressions with AND, OR, or NOT. AND and NOT limit the entries that pass the rule. In the case of AND, an entry must pass both rules; in the case of NOT, an entry must pass one rule and fail the other. Using OR increases the likelihood that an entry will pass the rule, because the entry only needs to pass one of the two rules separated by OR.

Access has some rules about the two field properties that it uses to validate data:

+ The **validation rule** cannot be longer than 2,048 characters.

+ The **validation text** cannot be longer than 255 characters.

You may want to use a different type of validation called record validation (as opposed to field validation, which is defined in the Field Properties). Record validation allows you to create a rule to prevent internal inconsistency in a record — for instance, you may want to check that the Ship Date is not before the Order Date. Record validation is defined on the Table Properties dialog box — to display it, display the table Design view and click the Properties button.

See also "Blocking Unwanted Data with an Input Mask," in this part.

Moving a Column in a Datasheet

Move a column heading (the entire column goes with it) in Datasheet view by dragging it. Follow these steps:

1. Click the field header of the column you want to move to select the column.

2. Click the field name a second time and drag the column to its new position.

The mouse pointer turns into the move pointer (as I call it), and a dark line appears where the column is going.

3. When the dark line is in the position you want the column in, release the mouse button.

Moving Around in a Datasheet

You can move around a datasheet in three ways: with the mouse, with keystrokes, and with the VCR buttons at the bottom of the datasheet window:

✦ Moving with the mouse: Click the cell in the datasheet where you want the cursor to be. You can also click the vertical and horizontal scroll bars to change the part of the datasheet that is displayed.

✦ Moving with keys: In addition to using arrows, Page Up and Page Down you can use these keystrokes to move around a datasheet:

Key to Press	Where It Takes You
Ctrl+PgUp	Left one screen
Ctrl+PgDn	Right one screen
Tab	Following field
Shift+Tab	Preceding field
Home	First field of the current record
End	Last field of the current record
Ctrl+↑	First record of the current field
Ctrl+↓	Last record of the current field
Ctrl+Home	First record of the first field (the top-left corner of the datasheet)
Ctrl+End	Last record of the last field (the bottom-right corner of the datasheet)
F5	Specified record (type a record number and press Enter to go to a specific record)

✦ Moving with VCR buttons: Use the VCR buttons at the bottom of the datasheet to move the cursor. When you know the record number you want, type it in the Record Number box and press Enter.

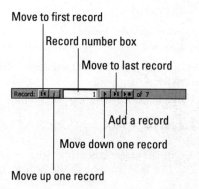

Move to first record

Record number box

Move to last record

Add a record

Move down one record

Move up one record

Naming and Renaming Fields

The rules for naming Access fields are simple:

+ Start with a letter or a number. (Actually, this isn't a hard and fast rule, but it's good practice.)

+ Don't use more than 64 characters.

If you may ever want to use your database in a real SQL environment (for example, move it out of Access to another database application), don't use spaces in field names.

Changing the name of a field before you finish designing a table is a hassle-free task.

To rename a field, follow these steps:

1. Double-click the field name.

Access selects the entire name.

2. Type a new name for the field.

Alternatively, you can edit the current name by pressing F2 to deselect the name but remain in edit mode. Then press the Backspace and Delete keys to remove unnecessary characters, and type in new characters.

3. Press Enter to enter the new name, or press Esc to cancel the renaming procedure.

If you need to change the name of a field after you use the field name in lookup lists, queries, forms, or reports, make sure you have the Name AutoCorrect feature on. When Name AutoCorrect is on, the name of the field will automatically be renamed in any queries, forms, or reports you have used it in. *See also* Part VIII.

Relating (Linking) Tables

Most databases consist of a number of tables. Each table contains a number of fields that are related. For instance, one table may contain customer information with fields for names, address, and phone number. Another table may contain customer orders with fields for data ordered and number of items ordered. Yet another table may contain detail information on the order with fields for the item number, description, and price. All of the tables contain related data, but Access doesn't know that until you link the tables by defining related fields. For example, a customer number field is used to link the customer information table to the customer order table, which means that the customer number field must appear in both tables. And an order number is used to link the customer order table to the order detail table.

Once tables are linked with related fields, you can create queries and reports that use fields from a number of tables. For instance, once I've defined related fields, I can create a report that lists customers and the items that they ordered — information that is found in two different tables. Telling Access about the relationships between tables is the key to making your relational database useful.

Pick your related fields carefully — make sure that both fields contain exactly the same type of data. Usually, a related field is the primary key in one table and simply information in the other table. A *primary key* is the field that uniquely identifies each record in the table.

Related fields must be the same data type, or the link will not work.

See also Part III for more information about key fields.

If you're creating a database, it's quite appropriate (and necessary) to link tables. If you are not the creator of the database, however, you should consult an expert before changing any relationships that the creator defined.

Types of relationships

Fields that appear in more than one table can be related in one of four ways. The four types of relationships are:

✦ **One-to-one:** A record in one table has exactly one related record in another table. For example, each record in a table that lists employees by name has exactly one related record in a table that lists employees by employee number, and each employee number refers to only one employee.

✦ **One-to-many:** One record in the first table has many related records in the second table. For example, one table that lists artists may have many related records in another table that lists CDs by artist.

✦ **Many-to-one:** This relationship is identical to one-to-many, except that you look at the relationship from the other side. For example, each record in a table that lists CDs by artist has only one related record in a table that lists artists, but many CDs may have the same artist.

✦ **Many-to-many:** This relationship is the most complicated type. A many-to-many relationship requires a linking table. For example, the item field in a table listing items by the stores that sell them has a many-to-many relationship to the item field in a table listing stores and the items they sell. An item may be sold by many stores, and many stores sell a particular item.

Creating and managing relationships

To define the relationships in your database:

1. Choose Tools⇨Relationships or click the Relationships button on the toolbar.

If no relationships are defined in the database, Access displays the Show Table dialog box, where you choose which tables with fields you want to use in relationships. If you already defined relationships in the database, Access displays the Relationships window.

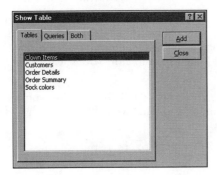

2. Add tables to the Relationships window by selecting them in the Show Table dialog box and clicking the Add button.

You can also add a table to the Relationships window by double-clicking the table name. You can select more than one table by selecting the first table and Ctrl+clicking the others. Then click the Add button.

3. Click the Close button to close the Show Table dialog box. If you need to display it again, click the Show Tables button on the toolbar.

4. Pick two related fields. Use the scroll bars to display the fields you want to link. Drag the field from one table and drop it on its related field in the second table.

If you drag the wrong field, just drop it on the gray background rather than dragging it to a field in a table. Then you're ready to start again.

When you release the mouse button, Access displays the Edit Relationships dialog box that details the nature of the relationship.

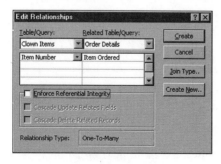

5. Make sure that the table and field names are correct; then click Create to tell Access to create the relationship.

If a field name is incorrect, you can change it by clicking the name of the field, clicking the arrow to display the drop-down list, and choosing another field name from the same table. If the relationship looks completely wrong, click Cancel and start over.

To reopen the Relationships dialog box after you've closed it, double-click the line joining two fields in the Edit Relationships window.

6. Repeat Steps 3 through 5 to create relationships between other fields.

Access automatically saves the relationships that you create. You can view the relationships in the Relationships window. You can print relationships by selecting File⇒Print Relationships from the menu when the Relationships window is active.

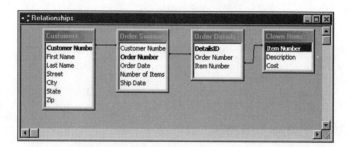

You may want to use the Enforce Referential Integrity check box on the Edit Relationships dialog box to help you avoid "orphan" data. In the case of the relationship between the Order Detail and Clown Items tables, an orphan record would be one in the Order Detail table with a item number in the Item Ordered field but with no matching value in the Item Number field of the Clown Items table. This orphan record means that an item number in an order has no corresponding descriptive information in the Clown Items table — in other words, an item number has been entered, but no such item exists. When referential integrity is enforced, an error message appears when an item number that doesn't exist in the Clown Items table is entered in the Order Detail table. When the Enforce Referential Integrity check box contains a check mark, Access adds symbols to the line representing the link to show the "one" and "many" sides of the relationship.

To delete a relationship, click the line that connects the two fields in the Relationships window and press Delete.

You can move tables around in the Relationships window so that the relationships are easy to understand; just drag the title bar of the table to move it. You can also size a table so that you can see more field names; just drag the border.

Saving a Table

Access automatically saves data entered in a table when you move to the next record. However, you do need to save the table design — the field definitions and formats. To save a table design, follow these steps:

1. Make sure the table is active.

If the table is active, the color of its title bar matches the color of the Access title bar. You can click a window to make it active.

 2. Click the Save button, press Ctrl+S, or choose File⇔Save.

You can also save a table by closing it. If you have made changes in a table since the last time you used it, when you close the table, Access asks whether you want to save it. Remember that the data is saved automatically each time you move to another field. What you need to save is the table design and the datasheet formatting.

Setting Field Size

For Text and Memo fields, use the Field Size option in the Field Properties pane of the table in Design view to limit input in the field to a specific number of characters. For Number data, the Field Size defines the type of number, and tells Access how much space is required to store each value.

The following are the Field Size options for numeric data:

Numeric Field Size Settings	What They Do
Byte	Allows values from 0 to 255 with no decimal places
Integer	Allows values from -32,768 to 32,767 with no decimal places
Long Integer	Allows values from about negative 2 billion to about positive 2 billion with no decimal places
Double	Allows really huge numbers, both positive and negative, with up to 15 decimal places
Single	Allows not-quite-as-huge numbers, both positive and negative, with up to seven decimal places

If you shorten the field size after entering data, you risk losing data when Access truncates entries longer than the new field size. The default field size for Text data, for example, is 50 characters. If you change the Field Size setting to 25, all entries longer than 25 characters are truncated to 25 characters. However, Access will warn you if you are going to lose data as a result of shortening the field length.

Sorting a Table

Your data may have been entered randomly, but it doesn't have to stay that way. Use the Sort commands (or buttons) to sort your data.

Before you sort, you have to know what you want to sort by. Do you want the Addresses table in order by last name, for example, or by zip code? When you know which field you want to sort by, sorting is a piece of cake.

You can sort in ascending order or descending order. *Ascending order* means that you start with the smallest number or the letter nearest the beginning of the alphabet, and work up from there. When you sort in ascending order, fields starting with *A* are at the top of the table, and fields starting with *Z* are at the bottom. *Descending order* is the opposite.

Follow these steps to sort a table in Datasheet view:

1. Select the field you want to sort by (sometimes called the *sort key*) by clicking the field name.

If you don't select the column (and you don't have to), Access uses the field the cursor is in as the sort key.

  2. Click the Sort Ascending or Sort Descending button, depending on which order you want to sort in.

If, for some strange reason, you prefer taking extra steps, you can use the menu. Choose Records⇨Sort⇨Sort Ascending or Records⇨Sort⇨Sort Descending.

Queries: Getting Answers from Your Data

Queries are one of the most commonly used and powerful features in Access. If the meat of your database is the data in tables, then queries are the muscle that let you get work done. Queries enable you to view subsets of your data. If your tables are linked, you can use a query to look at information from more than one table, and you can use a query to view a subset of information — perhaps you want to view account information only for overdue accounts. You can even use queries to create new calculated fields.

Part IV explains how to create queries to get information from one table or several tables. This part also explains how to define your queries so that you get the answer you're looking for.

In this part . . .

- ✔ Using queries to create calculated fields
- ✔ Creating action queries
- ✔ Creating crosstab queries
- ✔ Creating select queries
- ✔ Using wizards to create queries
- ✔ Using criteria in queries
- ✔ Using the Query by Example (QBE) grid

About Queries

Queries enable you to select specific data from one or more tables. Select queries are the most common type of queries used in Access — you may also use action queries. When you define a select query you choose which fields and records to display in the new datasheet by using the query grid in the query Design view. You can use select queries for analysis, or to filter data for use in forms or reports.

Action queries make changes to your data. Many of the skills you use to define select queries are used to define action queries.

Like tables, queries have two views: Design view and Datasheet view. In the Design view, you tell Access which fields tables you want to see, which tables they come from, and the criteria that have to be true for a record to appear on the resulting datasheet.

Criteria are tests that a record has to pass — for example, you may want to see only records with a value in the Amount field greater than 100. The criterion is that the value in the Amount field must be greater than 100.

In Datasheet view, you see the fields and records Access finds that meet your criteria.

A query doesn't store data — it just pulls data out of tables for you to look at. A query is *dynamic* — as you add to or change your data, the result of the query also changes. When you save your query, you're not saving the table that the query produces — you're just saving the query design so that you can ask the same question again.

Following are some kinds of queries:

✦ **Advanced Filter/Sort:** The Advanced Filter/Sort feature in Access is the simplest kind of query; it allows you to find and sort information from one table in the database. This option is available from the Datasheet view of a table by choosing Records⇨Filter⇨Advanced Filter/Sort.

✦ **Select:** A select query finds the data you want from one or more tables and displays it in the order in which you want it displayed. A select query can include criteria that tell Access to filter records and display only some of them.

✦ **Total:** These queries are similar to select queries, but they allow you to calculate a sum or some other aggregate (such as an average).

+ **Action:** Action queries change your data based on some set of criteria. Action queries can delete records, update data, append data from one or more tables to another table, and make a new table.

+ **Crosstab:** Most tables in Access, including ones generated by queries, have records down the side and field names across the top. Crosstab queries produce tables with the values from one field down the side and values from another field across the top of the table. A crosstab query performs a calculation — it sums, averages, or counts data that is categorized in two ways.

About Query Design View

Whichever kind of query you're using, you have to use query Design view to tell Access about the data you're looking for and where to look for it.

Do one of the following to display a query in Design view:

+ Click the Queries button in the Objects list on the Database window, select the query name, and click the Design button on the toolbar.

+ Ctrl+double-click the query name in the Queries view of the Database window.

Query by Example (QBE) pane

Pane divider

Field names   Table names   Table pane

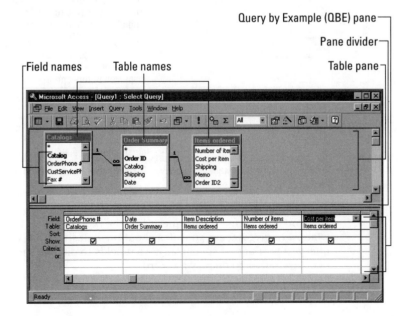

The following table explains what the buttons on the query Design view toolbar that are unique to queries do:

Toolbar Button	Button Name	What It Does
	View	Displays Datasheet view
	Save	Saves the query so that you can view the design and the query datasheet again
	Undo	Undoes your last undoable action (Many actions cannot be undone, so always keeping a backup is a good idea.)
	Select Query Type	Displays a drop-down list from which you can choose a query type: Select Query, Crosstab Query, Make-Table Query, Update Query, Append Query, or Delete Query
	Run	Runs the query (For a select query, clicking the Run button does the same thing as clicking the View button. When the query is an action query, the Run button performs the action. Use this button carefully.)
	Show Table	Displays the Show Table dialog box so that you can add tables to the query
	Totals	Displays the Total row in the query grid (Use the total row to tell Access what kind of calculation you want.)
All	Top Values	Limits the result of the query displayed in the datasheet to the number of records or the percentage of records displayed in this option
	Properties	Displays properties for the selected field or field list
	Build	Displays the Expression Builder dialog box (This button is "live" only when the cursor is in the Field or Criteria row.)
	Database Window	Displays the Database window

The top half of the window displays the tables containing fields that you want to use in the query. Use the bottom half of the window to give Access specifics about the datasheet you want the query to produce — specifically, what fields to display and how to decide whether to display a record.

Each row in the query grid has a specific purpose. Here's how to use each of them:

Query Grid Row	What It Does
Field	Provides the name of a field that you want to include in a query
Table	Provides the name of the table that the field comes from (This row is not always visible.)
Total	Performs calculations in your query (This row is not always visible — use the Totals button on the toolbar to display or hide it.)
Sort	Determines the sort order of the datasheet produced by the query
Show	Shows a field (If you want to use a field to determine which records to display on the datasheet, but not actually display the field, remove the check mark from the Show column for the field.)
Criteria	Tells Access the criteria for the field in the same column
Or	Use for additional criteria

See also "Limiting Records with Criteria Expressions," in this part.

Changing the size of query panes

You can change the size of the panes in Query view by clicking and dragging the pane divider. Just move the mouse pointer to the divider, where it changes shape; then click and drag to move the divider.

Changing the size of tables in the table pane

The tables in the table pane are really just little windows — you can move and size them in the same way that you move and size windows.

Change the size of a table window by moving the mouse pointer to the border of the window where it turns into a double-headed arrow; then click and drag the border to change the size of the window.

To move a table in the table pane, click and drag its title bar.

Navigating query Design view

You can work in query Design view by using the mouse (to click the pane that you want) and the scroll bars (to see parts of the view that don't fit on the screen). Or, if you prefer, you can use the keyboard to move around.

The following keys move you around query Design view:

Key	What It Does in the Table Pane	What It Does in the Query Pane
F6	Switches to the other pane	Switches to the other pane
Tab	Moves to the next table	Moves to the next row to the right
Shift + Tab	Moves to previous table	Moves to the next row to the left
Alt + ↓ or F4	Nothing	Displays the drop-down list (if the row has one)
PgDn	Displays more field names in the active table	Displays more OR criteria
Home	Moves to the top of field names	Moves to the first column in the grid

Adding a Select Query to the Database

The most frequently used type of query is called a *select query*. A select query displays fields from one or more tables based on criteria that you define.

Creating a select query from scratch

Here's how to create a select query from scratch:

1. Display Queries in the Database window.

2. Double-click the Create Query in Design View icon. Access displays query Design view and the Show Table dialog box.

3. Select the table(s) that contain fields you want to display in the query datasheet or use to create criteria by selecting the table(s) and then clicking the Add button in the Show Table dialog box. If you want to include a field generated by another query, you can add queries to a query by clicking the Queries or Both tab of the Show Table dialog box and double-clicking the query name.

4. Click the Close button in the Show Table dialog box.

5. Select the fields that you want to use in the query table. You can drag a field name to the design grid or double-click a field name to move it to the design grid. You can also use the drop-down Field and Table lists in the query grid to select the fields that you want to use.

6. Type the criteria that you want to use to create the query table. For example, if you want to see only records with values in the Order Numbers field over 100, type **>100** in the Criteria row of the column that contains the Order Numbers in a Field row. Or, if you want to see only those records whose Author field is Hemingway, type **Hemingway** in the Criteria row for the Author column.

See also "Calculating a Group of Data (Aggregate Calculations)," in this part.

7. Set the Sort and Show options to create your perfect query table.

See also "Sorting a Query," and "About Query Design View," in this part, for more information on using the Sort and Show rows in the query grid.

8. Click the View button to view the results of the query in a datasheet.

9. Save the query by clicking the Save button in the query's Design or Datasheet view.

If you're querying just one table, the easiest way to create the query is to select the table in the Database window and then click the New Object: Query button. (Query is not always what the New Object button is set to create — you may have to use the New Object button's drop-down list to choose Query.) Then select Design View in the New Query dialog box. Access displays Query Design view with the table that you selected displayed.

Using the Simple Query Wizard

The Simple Query Wizard does a great deal of the work of creating a query for you. The most basic query you can create with the Simple Query Wizard pulls together related data from different fields. The Simple Query Wizard is a terrific way to create some summary calculations from your data — such as how much was spent on an order or how many items were ordered.

The Simple Query Wizard gives you the option of creating a *summary* or *detail* query if the fields you choose for the query include both of the following:

✦ A field with values

✦ A field with repetitions, used to group the values

A *detail query* lists every record that meets your criteria. A *summary query* performs calculations on your data to summarize it. You can sum, average, count the number of values in a field, or find the minimum or maximum value in a field. A summary query creates new calculated fields that you can use in other queries or in reports.

For example, if you have a field that lists the amount spent and a field that lists the dates on which the money was spent, Access can create a summary query for you that sums the amount spent by date.

The Simple Query Wizard works like all wizards — it displays screens into which you enter information. *See* "Working with Wizards," in Part I.

Follow these steps to use the Simple Query Wizard to create a query:

1. Create a new query by displaying the Queries tab of the Database Window and clicking New. Access displays the New Query dialog box.

2. Select Simple Query Wizard and click OK. Access displays the first window of the query.

3. Use the Tables/Queries list box to choose the first table or query that you want to use fields from. When you select a table or query, fields from that object appear in the Available Fields list box.

4. Move fields you want to use in the query from the Available Fields list to the Selected Fields list by double-clicking a field name or by selecting the field name and then clicking the right-arrow button.

5. If you're using fields from more than one table or query, repeat Steps 3 and 4 to add fields from the additional tables or queries to the Selected Fields list.

6. Click Next after selecting all the fields you need for the query. Access displays the next window, which asks you if you want a detail or summary query. If summary calculations are not

possible with the fields you've chosen, Access skips this
window. For simple queries you may see the Finish window —
skip to Step 11.

7. Choose the type of query you want: Detail or Summary. If you
choose a Summary query, click the Summary Options button
to display the window where you tell the wizard how to
summarize each field.

Use the check boxes to indicate the new fields for Access to
create with this query. For example, if you want to add all the
values in the Cost per item field, click the Sum check box in
the row for the Cost per item field.

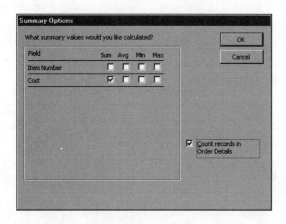

Don't overlook the Count check box(es) that may appear in
this window — selecting a Count check box tells the wizard to
create a field that counts the records within each grouping.

8. Click OK to leave the Summary Options window.

9. Click Next to view the next window. If you are summarizing
data, and if the fields being summarized can be grouped by a
Time/Date field, the wizard displays a window where you
choose the time interval the records should be grouped by.

For example, if you choose to sum a field that details check
amounts, and check amounts were entered in a record that
also contains a field telling the date each check was written,
you can choose to display total check amounts by Day, Month,
Quarter, or Year. Select the time interval to group by.

10. Click Next to see the final window.

11. Type a name for the query in the box at the top of the window.

12. Choose whether you want to Open the query to view information, which shows you the query in Datasheet view, or to Modify the query design, which shows you the query in Design view. If you want to see the help screen on working with a query, click the Display Help on Working With the Query check box.

13. Click Finish to view the query.

You can't tell the Simple Query Wizard about criteria. If you want to include criteria in your query, open the query created by the wizard in Design view and add the criteria.

See also "Limiting Records with Criteria Expressions," in this part.

Attaching a Table to a Query

In order to use a table's fields in a query, you have to "attach" the table to the query — that is, display the table name in the top half of the Query window.

It's a little odd that to add a table to a query, you use a dialog box called Show Table — but that's how it's done. Display the Show Table dialog box by doing any of the following things:

✦ Right-click the table part of query Design view and choose Show Table from the shortcut menu

✦ Click the Show Table button

✦ Choose Query⇨Show Table

After you display the Show Table dialog box, you add a table to the table pane of query Design view by doing either of the following things:

✦ Double-clicking the table name in the Show Table dialog box

✦ Selecting the table and then clicking the Add button

You can also add a query to the table pane if you want to use a field that was created or filtered by a query. Click the appropriate tab at the top of the Show Table dialog box to see all tables, all queries, or all tables and queries (Both).

When you have added all the tables that you need, click the Close button in the Show Table dialog box to work with the Query window.

To remove a table from a query, press Delete when a field in the table is highlighted. Deleting a table from a query is absurdly easy and can have damaging consequences for your query — when a table is deleted, all the fields from that table are deleted from the query grid. Take care when your fingers get close to the Delete key.

Calculating Summary Data for a Group of Data (Aggregate Calculations)

An *aggregate equation* is one that uses a bunch of records to calculate some result. For example, you may want to calculate the total cost of an order, count the number of orders that come in each day, or calculate an average dollar amount for all orders.

When you create an aggregate calculation, you tell Access to *group* data using a particular field. For example, if you want to know the number of orders that come in each day, you need to group the order data by date; that is, using the field that contains the date. If you want to count the number of orders for each item, then you need to group data using the field that contains the item name or number.

The easiest way to create aggregate calculations is to use the Summary option in the Simple Query Wizard. *See also* "Creating a Select Query," in this part.

Using the Total row

The Total row in the query grid enables you to aggregate data. To perform a total calculation on your data, you must select one of the options from the drop-down list for each field in the query grid.

The first step in creating a total is displaying the Total row in the query grid by clicking the Totals button. The Totals button appears to be raised when the Total row is not displayed and depressed when the Total row is displayed (you have to move the pointer to the button to see the 3-D effect).

When the Total row is displayed, you must select a setting in the Total row for each field in the query. The following table lists the choices for the Total row and how each works.

Total Row Choice	How It Works
Group By	Groups the values in this field so that like values are in the same group, allowing you to perform calculations on a group
Sum	Calculates the sum (total) of values in the field

Total Row Choice	How It Works
Avg	Calculates the average of values in the field (blanks are not included in the calculation)
Min	Finds the minimum value in the field
Max	Finds the maximum value in the field
Count	Counts the entries in the field (does not count blanks)
StDev	Calculates the standard deviation of values in the field
Var	Calculates the variance of values in the field
First	Finds the value in the first record in the field
Last	Finds the value in the last record in the field
Expression	Tells Access that you plan to type your own expression for the calculation
Where	Tells Access to use the field to limit the data included in the total calculation

Aggregating groups of records

To calculate aggregates, you must select one or more fields to group by. In the example, I want to calculate the total cost of an order, so I group by the fields defined in the Order Summary table that contains one record for each order.

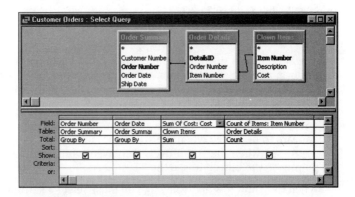

The Group By option in the Total row enables you to perform an aggregate calculation on a group of records. The result is a datasheet that has one row for each value in the field (with no repetitions) and a calculated field for the value.

Each field with an aggregate function (Sum, Avg, Min, Max, Count, StDev, Var, First, or Last) in the Total row is displayed as a calculated field in the datasheet that results from the query.

Order Number	Order Date	Sum Of Cost	Count of Items
1	10/1/98	$184.00	3
2	10/5/98	$227.00	2
3	10/6/98	$230.00	2
4	10/6/98	$310.00	2
5	10/14/98	$101.00	3
6	10/25/98	$285.00	2
7	11/1/98	$375.00	3
9	11/15/98	$80.00	3
10	11/14/98	$310.00	2
11	11/16/98	$160.00	1
12	11/20/98	$456.00	6
14	11/30/98	$40.00	1
15	12/3/98	$190.00	1

Record: |◄| ◄| 1 |►|►I|►*| of 13

Access creates new fields to hold the aggregate calculation. You can use these new fields in reports, forms, and other queries.

To create an aggregate calculation for grouped records, follow these steps:

1. Create a new query in Design view.

> *See also* "Creating a Select Query," in this part.

2. From the Show Tables window, choose the tables that you need fields from and add them to the query. Close the Show Tables window.

3. Double-click the field you want to group data by to display it in the query grid.

4. Choose Group By from the drop-down list in the Total row. If the Total row doesn't appear in the query grid, click the Totals button on the toolbar.

5. Move the fields that you want to use in aggregate calculations to the query grid.

6. Choose the type of calculation that you want for each field from the drop-down list in the Total row.

To perform more than one type of calculation on a field, put the field in more than one column in the query grid and specify a different type of calculation in each Total row.

You can also group by more than one field. If you want aggregate information about people who have the same last name and live at the same address, you can use the Group By setting in both the last name field and the address field.

If you don't use the Group By option for any of the fields in the query grid, the result of any aggregation is the same — the "group" that you aggregate includes all records.

Limiting records to aggregate

You can use the Criteria and the Total rows together to limit the records used in the aggregate calculation or to limit the records displayed after the calculations are performed.

You have to be careful, though, to make sure that Access does exactly what you want it to do. Here are some tips on using the Criteria and Total rows in one query:

✦ If you use Criteria in a Group By field, you limit the data that Access uses for the aggregate calculation. In other words, Access first finds the records that meet the criterion and then performs the aggregate calculation on just those records.

✦ If you use Criteria in a field with an aggregate function (Sum, Avg, Min, Max, Count, StDev, Var, First, or Last), Access uses the criteria to limit the result of the calculation. It first does the calculation and then selects the results that meet the criteria for the datasheet.

✦ Use the Where option in the Total row when you want to limit the records used for the calculation by using a field that is not a Group By field. When you use the Where option, you can also use a criterion. The Where option limits the records used for the aggregate calculation to those that pass the criterion for the field — think of it as meaning "Limit the records to Where this criterion is true."

When you use the Where option, you use it only to limit records — Access knows this and turns off the Show check box. In fact, you can't show a field used with the Where option in the Total row. If you want to display a field used with the Where option, use the same field in another column of the query grid with the Group By option in the Total row.

Creating your own expression for an aggregate calculation

You're not limited to the aggregate functions Access provides to perform a calculation in a query — you can write your own expression, instead. To write your own expression for an aggregate calculation, choose Expression in the Total row and type the expression into the Field row of the grid.

To create your own expression, follow these steps:

1. Move your cursor to the Field row of a blank column in the query grid.

2. Type the name of the new field that you are creating, followed by a colon.

3. Type the expression in the Field row after the colon.

4. Select Expression in the Total row of the new field.

See also "Calculating Fields (Building Expressions)," in this part, for more information on creating expressions.

Calculating Fields (Building Expressions)

When you're creating your database, don't waste your time dragging out your calculator, doing the math yourself, and then typing in the result. Instead, tell Access to perform any calculations for you. The work gets done faster, and the result is always up-to-date — even if you later add, delete, or change records.

You can add calculations to queries and reports by typing an expression, sometimes called a *formula,* which tells Access exactly what to calculate. In a query, you put the expression in the Field row of one column of the query grid.

Most expressions include some basic elements, such as field names, values, and operators. Field names must be enclosed in brackets. Following is an example of an expression that calculates profit using fields called "Revenues" and "Expenses":

```
Profit: [Revenues] - [Expenses]
```

The name of the new field appears first, followed by a colon. The names of existing fields are enclosed in square brackets.

You can also use values in an expression, as follows:

```
Retail Cost: [Wholesale Cost] * 1.50
```

You aren't limited to performing calculations with values; you can also perform calculations with dates, times, and text data. *See* "Using functions," later in this section, for more information on working with non-numeric data.

Some types of data must be enclosed between special characters so that Access knows what kind of data it is. The following table tells you how to use different elements in an expression.

Type of Data in an Expression	*How It Should Look*
Text	"Massachusetts"
Date/time	#15-Jan-97#
Field name	[Cost]

The following are the basic steps to take to add a calculated field to a query:

1. In the query grid, click the Field row of a blank column.

2. Type the name of the new field, followed by a colon. If you don't give the new field a name, Access names it for you — with something unintelligible, such as Expr1. If you're writing an expression to calculate cost and you want to call the new field Total Cost, type **Total Cost:**.

3. Type the expression you want Access to calculate.

In the following query, the new field is called Total Cost, and the expression to calculate Total Cost follows the colon.

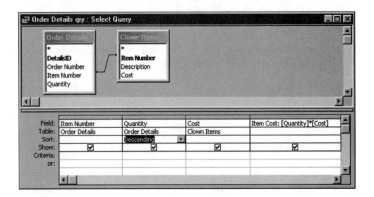

 4. To see the result, click the View button.

Item Ordered	Quantity	Cost	Item Cost
Twirling Paper Parasol	4	$10.00	$40.00
Twirling Paper Parasol	2	$10.00	$20.00
Juggling clubs (1)	2	$15.00	$30.00
Clown Socks	2	$18.00	$36.00
Orange Wig	2	$24.00	$48.00
Two-tone neon pant clown suit	1	$150.00	$150.00
Sword through Neck illusion	1	$120.00	$120.00
Newspaper Dove Vanish	1	$45.00	$45.00
Unicycle	1	$160.00	$160.00
Disecte wrist chopper	1	$125.00	$125.00

Record: 14 ◄ | 1 | ► ►I ►* | of 33

After you create the new field, you can use it in other queries and in other calculations.

You can display a zoom window for your expression that allows you to see the whole expression. To display the contents of a cell in a zoom window, position your cursor in the cell and press Shift+F2. (This works in a table, too.)

Using a parameter in an expression

You may want to change the value in a criteria or expression without having to rewrite the expression in query Design view each time. For instance, you may want to see the names of customers who ordered a particular product. You can do so by creating a parameter query. When you run a parameter query, Access displays the Enter Parameter Value dialog box and tells you the name of the field for which it needs a value.

Enter the value of the field name listed, and click OK to see the datasheet.

You can use this to your advantage — for instance, if you're in retail and want to be able to calculate the markup for a variety of your products, first, make sure you don't name any of your fields Markup, then create an expression that includes [Markup]. Then, each time you run the query, you get the Enter Parameter Value dialog box and can enter a different markup value.

Using operators in calculations

Access has a slew of operators. The operators that you're most likely to have worked with are the *logical* and *relational* operators, which result in a true or false result. However, Access also has operators that you use in calculations.

Mathematical operators work with numbers. The following table lists mathematical operators and what they do.

Mathematical Operator	What It Does
*	Multiplies
+	Adds
−	Subtracts
/	Divides
^	Raises to a power

Creating a text field with an expression

Text data are often called *strings* by technoids. Text/string operators work with text and memo fields. You can add two strings together by using "&," the string operator that concatenates (adds together) strings. Access also has functions that work with strings.

You can use different types of data in an expression that results in a text string; you're not limited to text data. You may want to include a numeric value or a date in a string, for example. Using the "&" operator converts data to a string, so the final result is a string.

Using functions

Functions allow you to create calculations that would be difficult or impossible to perform with operators. The following are the six major categories of functions that you're likely to use:

✦ **Conversion:** Convert one type of data to another (numeric to string, for example).

✦ **Date/Time:** Work with time and date data.

✦ **Financial:** Perform financial calculations, such as calculating the internal rate of return (IRR) or the net present value (NPV).

✦ **Mathematical:** Perform mathematical calculations, such as calculating the square root, sine, or log.

✦ **Text:** Manipulate text or string expressions.

✦ **Domain:** Calculate aggregate statistics on a set of records.

You use all these functions in a similar way — use the name of the function followed by the argument or arguments in parentheses. *Arguments* are what the function uses to perform its calculation. The function SQR( ), for example, takes the square root of a number, so the following expression produces the square root of the value in the field called Hypotenuse:

```
SQR([Hypotenuse])
```

Note: Although I show function names in all capital letters, you can use any combination of capital and lowercase.

Remember that the argument has to be enclosed in parentheses, and a field name used in an expression has to be enclosed in square brackets. For the rules on using field names, dates, and strings in expressions, *see* the introduction to this topic, "Calculating Fields (Building Expressions)."

The best way to see the Access functions and to use them in building expressions is to use the Functions folder in the Expression Builder.

Using the Expression Builder

When you know what you want your expression to do, but you're not sure how to write it so that Access understands it, you may find the Expression Builder useful. The Expression Builder can help you avoid errors in an expression, but it can't help you figure out how to create the calculation you need. Your formulas look just as complicated in the Expression Builder as they do when you type them directly in the Field row of the query grid.

To use the Expression Builder to write a calculation, follow these steps:

1. Click the Field row in the column where you want to add a calculation.

2. Click the Build button in the toolbar. Access displays the Expression Builder.

Objects contained in object selected in first box

┌Operators you can click │ Expression box

Expression Builder	? X

OK
Cancel
Undo
Help

+ - / * & = > < <> And Or Not Like ( ) Paste Help

All Items Ordered	Date	<Value>

- Tables
  - Catalogs
  - Items ordered
  - Order Summary
- Queries
- Forms
- Reports
- Functions
- Constants
- Operators
- Common Expressions

Date
Catalog
Item Description
Number of items
Cost per item

└Database objects

More detail about items selected in first two boxes

The Build button is unavailable (grayed out) except when the cursor is in a Field row or a Criteria row — the only two rows in the query grid that allow an expression. (You can use the Expression Builder to build a criteria expression as well as to build an expression for a calculated field.)

The Expression Builder allows you to choose field names, operators, and parentheses (to determine the order of calculation) to build an expression. The Expression Builder takes care of the funny characters that Access needs in an expression, such as the square brackets around field names. The Expression Builder also lists all of Access's operators and functions, so that you don't have to type them yourself and risk typos. But using the Expression Builder is not for the faint of heart — you may find typing simple expressions directly into the query grid easier than trying to figure out all the boxes in the Expression Builder.

Here are some ways to use the Expression Builder:

✦ You can type directly in the Expression box — just click it and start typing.

✦ You can put operators in the Expression box by clicking the button that shows the operator you want to use in your expression.

✦ You can put an element from the lower boxes in the Expression box by double-clicking it or by highlighting it and then clicking the Paste button.

✦ You can undo the last thing that you did to the expression by clicking the Undo button.

✦ When you add a field name from a lower box to the expression, Access includes the name of the table that the field comes from, as follows:

```
[table name]![field name]
```

✦ You can expand any folder in the first lower box that has a plus sign (+) by double-clicking the folder.

✦ When you click an object (such as a table, query, form, or report name), the names of the fields used in that object appear in the center lower box.

✦ If you put the names of two fields in the Expression box without an operator between them, Access adds a generic operator (<<Expr>>). To put a real operator in the expression, select the generic operator and then click an operator button. Access replaces <<Expr>> with the operator you click.

✦ All Access functions are available from the Expression Builder. Double-click the Functions folder in the first lower box and then click Built-in Functions. Access displays categories of functions in the second box. Click a category to see specific functions in the third box. Click a function; Access displays an example of how it should be used at the bottom of the dialog box.

✦ Access provides some common expressions in the Common Expressions folder, which appears at the bottom of the first box.

Click the OK button to close the Expression Builder and put the expression in the query.

Changing the Format of a Query Field

To change the format of a calculated field, follow these steps:

1. In query Design view, right-click anywhere in the column that contains the field you want to format.

2. Choose Properties from the shortcut menu. Access displays the Field Properties dialog box.

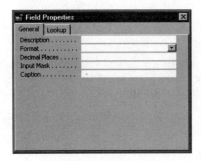

3. Display the drop-down list for Format to display the format options.

4. Choose the format option that you want from the drop-down list.

The options in the Field Properties dialog box are exactly the same as the options that appear in the Field Properties pane of table Design view, and you can use them in exactly the same way. However, when you format a field in a query you affect how that field appears only in the query datasheet. *See also* "Customizing Fields Using the Field Properties Pane," in Part III.

Creating Action Queries

Action queries are a way to make global corrections to your database. Before you delve into the complexities of an action query, though, you should consider whether you can fix the problem by using the much simpler Find and Replace dialog box to find and replace data. *See* "Finding Data in a Table," in Part III, for more information on the Find dialog box. You can use the Find and Replace dialog box in a datasheet created by a query, and if you change the data in the query, the table holding the underlying data will reflect the change.

Action queries differ significantly from select queries. A select query shows you data that meet your criteria; an action query does something with the data that meet your criteria.

You may need to create an action query if you want to do any of the following things:

✦ Delete some records *(delete query)*

✦ Append data from one table to another table *(append query)*

✦ Update information in some records *(update query)*

✦ Create a new table from data stored in other tables *(make-table query)*

When you create a query by choosing Design View in the New Query dialog box (*see* "Creating a Select Query" for more information), Access automatically creates a select query.

To change the query type, do either of the following things:

✦ Click the arrow next to the Query Type button and choose the query type that you want.

✦ Choose the type of query you want from the Query menu. (You can choose Query⇨Make Table Query, Query⇨ Update Query, Query⇨Append Query, or Query⇨Delete Query to create an action query.)

Note that the term *action query* actually represents a category of query, not a specific query. In other words, there is more than one type of action query. The four queries just introduced are, collectively, known as action queries.

When you work with a select query, the View and Run buttons do the same thing. When you work with an action query, the View and Run buttons do completely different jobs:

✦ The View button displays Datasheet view, which is a good way to preview what you're going to do with the action query.

✦ The Run button executes the action — it deletes or changes data in your database. You cannot undo the action after you click the Run button in an action query, so be very sure that the query is set up correctly before you run it.

When you double-click an action query in the Database window or use another method to open a query, you're telling Access to run the query (not just to show it). Access warns you that you are about to do whatever it is you're about to do — update records, delete records, or whatever — and gives you a chance to change your mind. If all you want to do is work on the design of the query, make sure that you select the query and click the Design button.

It's easy to recognize action queries in the Database window, because their icons are a little different from the icons select queries have — all action-query icons have an exclamation point.

You may want to make a copy of the table(s) affected by the action query before you run it. *See also* "Copying a Database Object," in Part VIII. In addition, you can use these methods to avoid accidentally acting on the wrong record:

➤ The really safe method is to first create a select query, to ensure that the records selected are the records that you actually want to perform the action on.

➤ The fairly-safe-but-not-absolutely-foolproof method is to set up your query and then click the View button to see Datasheet view. The datasheet shows you the data that the query has found to act on. Be careful to use the View button rather than the Run button, which actually performs the action.

Update queries

You can use an *update query* to change a pile of data at the same time — to raise prices by 10 percent, for example, or to change the earthquake risk of all your New Hampshire insurance clients from low to medium.

To create an update query, follow these steps:

1. Create a new query in Design view. Access displays query Design View and the Show Table dialog box.

See also "Creating a Select Query," in this part.

2. Add the tables that you plan to update or that you need to use fields from to establish the update criteria.

3. Close the Show Table dialog box.

4. Change the query type to Update Query by clicking the arrow next to the Query Type button and choosing Update Query from the drop-down list or by choosing Query⇨Update Query.

5. Put fields in the query grid.

Add fields that you want to see in the datasheet, that you want to use with criteria to tell Access exactly what to update, and that you actually want to update.

6. Add the criteria to tell Access how to choose the records to update.

7. Use the Update To row to tell Access how to update the data. This query finds records where the state is equal to "NH" and changes the value of the field Earthquake Risk for those records to Medium.

 The easiest update is to change one value to another by simply typing the new value in the Update To box. More complex updates include expressions that tell Access exactly how to update the field. You can use the Expression Builder to help you build an expression for the Update To setting; just click the Build button. *See also* "Calculating Fields (Building Expressions)."

 8. Click the View button. Access displays the datasheet with the records the query found that match your criteria. If the data is not correct, return to Design view to correct the fields and criteria.

 You can display only those fields in the datasheet that the update query is actually working with; in an update query, every field displayed in the datasheet has either an expression in the Criteria row or a value or expression in the Update To row in the query grid. If you want to get a fuller picture of the records you're updating (see the data for all the fields, for example), you can change the query type back to Select, add additional fields, and view the datasheet that your criteria produces. When you change the query type back to Update, the Update To options you added are still there. You need to remove any additional fields from the query grid before you run the update.

9. Run the update by clicking the Run button. Access warns you that after the records are updated, you can't undo the changes.

10. Click Yes to update the data.

11. Check the tables with affected fields to see whether the update query worked correctly.

12. Delete the query if you won't be using it again; save it if you will need it again.

Make-table queries

A *make-table query* can be useful if you need to make a new table to export or to serve as a backup. You can also simply make a copy of a table or query. *See* "Finding Your Way Around a Database," in Part II.

To create a table with a make-table query, follow these steps:

1. Create a new select query that produces the records you want in a new table. Access copies the records to the new table.

See also "Creating a Select Query," in this part.

2. Change the query type to make-table by clicking the arrow next to the Query Type button and choosing Make-Table Query from the drop-down list or by choosing Query⇨ Make-Table Query. Access immediately displays the Make-Table dialog box.

3. In the Table Name box, type the name of the table that you're creating.

4. Click OK. Access displays Query Design view. A make-table query has the same rows in the query grid as a select query.

5. Click the View button to see the records that Access will copy to the new table. You may need to return to the Design view to edit the query until all the records you want in the new table appear in the datasheet when you click the View button.

6. Click the Run button to create the new table. Access asks whether you're sure, because you won't be able to undo your changes.

7. Click <u>Y</u>es to create the new table.

8. Check the new and old tables to make sure that you got what you need in the new table.

Append queries

An *append query* takes data from one or more tables or queries in your database and adds it to an existing table. As with other queries, you can use criteria to tell Access exactly which data to append.

Cutting and pasting is often an easier way to append records from one table to another. *See* "Cutting, Copying, and Pasting," in Part VIII, for more information.

Access gets a little picky about data that you append using an append query, especially when it comes to the primary key field. You must follow these rules when appending records to another table:

✦ Data that you want to append must have unique values in the field that is the primary key field in the table to which the data is being added. If the field is blank, or if the same value already exists in the table, Access does not append the records.

✦ If the primary key field in the table to which the data is being appended is an AutoNumber field, do not append data in that field — Access automatically generates new numbers in the AutoNumber field for the new records and old values cannot be appended.

✦ The data type of each field that you're appending must match the data type of fields in the table to which they're being added.

To create an append query, follow these steps:

1. Create a select query that produces the records that you want to add to another table.

See also "Creating a Select Query," in this part.

2. Change the query type to Append by clicking the arrow next to the Query Type button and choosing <u>A</u>ppend Query from the drop-down list or by choosing Query⇨<u>A</u>ppend Query.

Access immediately displays the Append dialog box.

3. Choose the table to which you want to append the records.

You can display the names of all the tables in the open database by displaying the Table Name drop-down list.

You can add the records to a table in another database, but you have to know the exact name of the database file, including the folder structure because there is no option to browse to find the file.

4. Click OK. Access returns you to the query design. The title bar of the query Design view window tells you that you're working with an append query. The query grid has an extra row: the Append To row. Access automatically fills in the Append To row with the names of the fields in the table you're appending records to, if the field names match the names of the fields you're appending.

5. If some of the fields don't have field names in the Append To row, display the drop-down list in the Append row and select the name of the field you want to append to. When you're finished, check each column to ensure that:

- The Field row contains the name of the field that contains data that you want to append to another table.

- The Table row contains the name of the table that contains the data.

- The Append To row contains the name of the field that the data will be appended to.

6. Click the Run button to run the append query. Access tells you that you're about to append rows and that you won't be able to undo the changes.

7. Click Yes to run the query.

Access adds the records to the table you specified. You now have the same information in two tables.

8. Save the query if you think that you'll use it again; otherwise, close it without saving.

9. Check your results. Check the table you appended to as well as the table you were appending from to make sure that Access copied all the records you wanted.

Delete queries

A *delete query* enables you to select your fields and add criteria in the same way that a select query does, but instead of displaying the records that the query finds, a delete query deletes them.

Delete queries are dangerous because they actually delete data from the tables in your database. Always make sure that you have a backup before you run a delete query. You may want to back up the whole database or just the tables affected by the delete query. *See also* "Copying a Database Object" and "Backing Up Your Database" in Part VIII, for more information.

When you tell Access to create a delete query, the Show row in the query grid is replaced by the Delete row. The Delete row has a drop-down list with two options:

+ **Where:** Tells Access to use the criteria for the field to determine which records to delete.

+ **From:** Displays the field when you view the datasheet for the query. You can choose the From option only when you use the * choice in the Field row to include all fields from a table. Viewing all fields from a table in the datasheet gives you a more complete picture of the data you're deleting; otherwise, all you see in the datasheet are the values from the fields that you include in the query grid with criteria rather than the entire record that the delete query will delete when you run it.

Here's how to create a delete query:

1. In Design view, create a new query that produces the records you want to delete. Access displays the query Design view and the Show Tables dialog box.

See "Creating a Select Query," in this part.

2. Add to the query all tables with data you want to delete.

3. Close the Show Tables dialog box.

4. Change the query type to Delete Query by clicking the down arrow next to the Query Type button and choosing Delete Query from the drop-down list or by choosing Query⇨ Delete Query.

When you change the query type from select to delete, Access replaces the Sort row of the query grid with the Delete row.

5. Drag the asterisk from the first table to the query grid. Repeat for any other tables you're using in the table grid. Access puts the asterisk — the symbol for all fields from a table — in the query grid. Notice that the value in the Delete row is From. This value tells Access to display the fields in the datasheet but not to use them to determine the data to delete.

6. Put the fields you're using to tell Access which records to delete in the query grid. When you add a single field to the query grid, Access gives it the Where option in the Delete row. The delete query uses the Criteria row of fields with the Where option to determine which records to delete.

7. Type the criteria. If you want to delete records in which the Cost Per Item field is greater than 100, for example, type >**100** in the Criteria row of the Cost Per Item column.

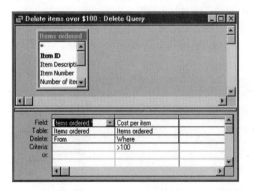

 8. Click the View Datasheet button to see the records that the delete query will delete when you run it. If you see data in the datasheet that shouldn't be deleted, or if data that you want to delete is missing, you need to correct the design of the query before you run it. Remember that a delete query deletes entire records.

 9. Return to Design view by clicking the View Design button.

 10. Run the query by clicking the Run button. Access deletes the data that you saw in Datasheet view — and it's gone for good!

You can delete records from related tables, but the relationships must be defined, and you need to check two options in the Relationships dialog box for each specific join: the Enforce Referential Integrity option and the Cascade Delete Related Fields option. Display the Relationships dialog box by double-clicking the line that connects two tables in Relationships view. *See also* "Relating (Linking) Tables," in Part II.

Creating a Crosstab Query

A *crosstab query* is a specialized kind of query for displaying summarized data. Instead of creating a table with rows showing record data and columns showing fields, you can use a crosstab query table to use data from one field for the row labels and data from another field for column labels. The result is a more compact, spreadsheet-like presentation of your data.

See also "Calculating Summary Data for a Group of Data (Aggregate Calculations)," in this part.

You may have a table in which Date and Class Level information are repeated, as shown in the following figure.

Date	Class Level	Time	# attendees
9/15/96	Beginner	9:00:00 AM	9
9/15/96	Intermediate	1:00:00 PM	5
9/15/96	Advanced	3:00:00 PM	5
9/15/96	Intermediate	5:00:00 PM	8
9/22/96	Beginner	9:00:00 AM	8
9/22/96	Intermediate	1:00:00 PM	4
9/29/96	Beginner	9:00:00 AM	5
9/29/96	Intermediate	1:00:00 PM	7
9/29/96	Advanced	3:00:00 PM	8
10/6/96	Beginner	9:00:00 AM	15
10/6/96	Intermediate	1:00:00 PM	6
10/6/96	Beginner	5:00:00 PM	7
10/20/96	Beginner	9:00:00 AM	17
10/20/96	Intermediate	1:00:00 PM	10
10/20/96	Advanced	3:00:00 PM	7
10/27/96	Beginner	9:00:00 AM	16
10/27/96	Intermediate	1:00:00 PM	11
11/3/96	Beginner	9:00:00 AM	10
11/3/96	Intermediate	1:00:00 PM	9
11/3/96	Advanced	3:00:00 PM	9

A crosstab query enables you to see this information in a more compact form, with the dates being the row labels, and the class levels being the column labels.

Date	Beginner	Intermediate	Advanced
9/15/96	9	13	5
9/22/96	8	4	
9/29/96	5	7	8
10/6/96	22	6	
10/20/96	17	10	7
10/27/96	16	11	
11/3/96	10	9	9
11/10/96	11	5	
11/17/96	15	16	
11/24/96	16	12	
12/1/96	12	8	5
12/8/96	11	9	
12/15/96	22	11	
12/22/96	11	10	

Classes_Crosstab1 : Crosstab Query

Record: 1 of 14

Using query Design view to create a crosstab query

A simple crosstab query has three fields — one used for row headings (Date, for example), one used for column headings (Class Level, for example), and one that contains the data that you want to appear in the cells of the table (number of students, for example). The third field is called the Value field, and you can tell Access how to summarize your data in the crosstab table by choosing from these choices: Sum, Avg, Min, Max, Count, StDev, Var, First, or Last. *See also* "Calculating a Group of Data (Aggregate Calculations)," in this part, for more information on aggregating fields.

Here's how to create a simple crosstab query:

1. Display the Queries view in the Database window.

2. Double-click the Create Query in Design View icon. Access displays the New Query window.

3. Select Design View from the New Query window and click OK. Access displays the Query Design view and the Show Table dialog box.

4. Double-click the tables or queries you want to use to create the crosstab query to add them to the table pane of the Design view.

   See also "Creating a Select Query," in this part.

5. Close the Show Table dialog box.

6. Change the query type to Crosstab by clicking the arrow next to the Query Type button and choosing Crosstab Query from the drop-down list. You can also choose Query⇨Crosstab Query. Access displays an additional row called Crosstab in the query grid. You use the Crosstab row to tell Access how to build the crosstab table.

7. Put the field you want Access to use for row labels in the grid by double-clicking it.

8. Display the Crosstab options for the field by clicking the down arrow in the Crosstab row. Choose Row Heading from the drop-down list.

9. Put the field you want Access to use for column labels in the grid by double-clicking it in the Table pane.

10. Display the Crosstab options for the field by clicking the down arrow in the Crosstab row. Choose Column Heading from the drop-down list.

11. In the Table pane, double-click the field containing the values you want aggregated in your Crosstab query to put it in the grid. This field provides the values that fill up the crosstab table.

12. Display the Crosstab options for the field by clicking the down arrow in the Crosstab row. Choose Value from the drop-down list.

13. In the column that contains the Value field, choose the option to summarize the data from the drop-down list in the Total row. *See also* "Calculating a Group of Data (Aggregate Calculations)," in this part, for more information on the options in the Total row.

When you finish, your query Design view should look something like this:

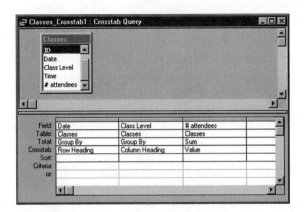

Using the Crosstab Query Wizard

The Crosstab Query Wizard provides an automated way to create a crosstab query.

The Crosstab Query Wizard works only with one table or query. If the fields you want to use in the crosstab query are not in one table, you have to create a query that combines those fields in one query before you use the Crosstab Query Wizard.

Start the Crosstab Query Wizard by following these steps:

1. Display the Queries in the Database window. Access displays the names of any queries you have in your database.

2. Click the New button. Access displays the New Query dialog box.

3. Select the Crosstab Query Wizard and click OK. Access starts the Crosstab Query Wizard.

The Crosstab Query Wizard works like other wizards; it asks you questions in the form of dialog-box options. To move to the next wizard screen, click the Next button. To go back to the preceding screen, click the Back button. *See also* "Working with Wizards," in Part I.

The Crosstab Query Wizard asks you for the following information:

✦ The table or query you want to use to create the crosstab table

✦ The field you want to use for row headings

◆ The field you want to use for column headings

◆ The field you want to summarize by using the row and column headings

◆ How you want to summarize the field (count the entries, add them together, average them, and so on)

◆ Whether you want Access to sum each row (Access adds a Sum of *Field Name* column to the table to display the result)

Displaying or Hiding Table Names

You can view table names for each field in the query grid through the Table row, or you can choose not to see the Table row.

To make the Table row appear or disappear, do either of the following things:

◆ Right-click the grid and choose Table <u>N</u>ames from the shortcut menu.

◆ Choose <u>V</u>iew⇨Table <u>N</u>ames (to turn off the check mark).

Editing a Query

You can do a few things in a query to edit it — you can move the columns around, delete a column, or delete all the entries in the design grid.

To do any of those things, though, you first have to select the column in the grid by clicking the column selector — the gray block at the top of each column in the grid.

Column selector

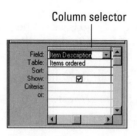

Following are some things you may want to do to make your query better:

When You Want to . . .	Here's What to Do
Move a column	Click the column selector to select the column, click a second time, and then drag the column to its new position.
Delete a column	Click the column selector to select the column; then press the Delete key to delete the column.
Delete all columns	Choose Edit⇨Clear Grid.
Insert a column	Drag a field from the table pane to the column in the grid where you want to insert it. Access inserts an extra column for the new field.
Change the displayed name	Use a colon between the display name and the actual name of the field in the Field row *(display name: field name)*.

Filtering a Table with Advanced Filter/Sort

The easiest kind of query to create is one that filters records in only one table. You perform this simple query by using the Advanced Filter/Sort command.

Follow these steps:

1. Open the table you want to filter in Datasheet view.

2. Choose Records⇨Filter⇨Advanced Filter/Sort. Access displays the Filter window, which has two parts, just like the query Design view.

3. Click the first field you want to use to filter the table and drag it to the Field row of the first column of the grid in the bottom half of the window. Instead of dragging a field, you can choose a field from the Field drop-down list.

4. Click the Criteria row in the first column and type the criteria to limit the records you see.

For example, if you want to see only items that cost more than $10, put the Cost per Item field in the Field row of the first column, and type **>10** in the Criteria row.

See also "Limiting Records with Criteria Expressions," in this part.

5. Repeat Steps 3 and 4 to add other fields and criteria to the grid.

6. (Optional) Choose a field by which to sort the resulting table. Set a sort order by displaying the drop-down list for the Sort row in the column containing the field you want to sort by — choose Ascending or Descending. This option tells Access to sort the table that results from the advanced filter in ascending or descending order, using the field listed in the same column as the sort key.

7. When you finish creating all the criteria you need, click the Apply Filter button to see the resulting table. Access displays all the fields in the original table, but it filters the records and displays only those that meet the criteria.

You can do several things with the resulting table:

✦ **Save it:** If you want to save your advanced filter, you have to save it in Design view. After you apply the filter, return to Design view by choosing Record⇨Filter⇨Advanced Filter/Sort and click the Save As Query button to save the advanced filter. You can get to the filter after it's saved through the Queries tab of the Database window.

✦ **Filter it:** Use the filter buttons and Record⇨Filter to filter the table even more.

✦ **Print it:** Click the Print button.

✦ **Sort it:** The best way to sort is to use the Sort row in the design grid. But you can use the Sort Ascending or Sort Descending buttons to sort the query-result table by the field that the cursor is in.

✦ **Fix it:** Choose Record⇨Filter⇨Advanced Filter/Sort to display the Design view to fix the criteria or other information in the grid.

✦ **Add data to it:** Add data to the table by clicking the New Record button and typing the data.

✦ **Edit data:** Edit data the same way that you do in the datasheet and press F2.

✦ **Delete records:** You can delete entire records if you want — click the record you want to delete and click the Delete Record button.

✦ **Toggle between the filtered table and the full table:** Click the Apply Filter button. If you're looking at the full table, clicking the Apply Filter button displays the filtered table (according to the last filter that you applied). If you're looking at the filtered table, clicking the Apply Filter button displays the full table.

Inserting Fields in a Query Grid

You can move a field from the table pane to the query grid in three easy ways:

✦ Double-click the field name. Access moves the field to the first open column in the grid.

✦ Drag the field name from the table pane to the field row of an unused column in the query grid.

✦ Use the drop-down list in the Field row of the query grid to choose the field you want. If you use this method with a multiple-table query, you may find it easier to choose the table name from the drop-down Table list before selecting the field name. If you don't have the Table row in your query grid, *see* "Displaying or Hiding Table Names" in this part.

You can put all the field names from one table into the query grid in two ways:

✦ Put one field name in each column of the grid: If you have criteria for all the fields, you can put one field name in each column of the query grid in just two steps. Double-click the table name where it appears in the table pane of the Design view to select all the fields in the table. Then drag the selected names to the grid. When you release the mouse button, Access puts one name in each column.

✦ Put all the field names in one column: This method is useful if you want to find something that could be in any field or if you have one criterion for all the fields in the table. The asterisk appears above the first field name in each Table window. Drag the asterisk to the grid to tell Access to include all field names in one column. The asterisk is also available as the first choice in the drop-down Field list — it appears as `TableName.*`.

Limiting Records with Criteria Expressions

Criteria enable you to limit the data that the query displays. Although you can use a query to see data from related tables together in one record, the power of queries is that you can filter your data to see only records that meet certain criteria. You use the Criteria and Or rows in the query grid to tell Access exactly which records you want to see.

Access knows how to *query by example* (QBE). In fact, the grid in
Design view is sometimes called the QBE grid. QBE makes creating
criteria easy. If you tell Access what you're looking for, Access
goes out and finds it. For example, if you want to find values equal
to 10, the Criteria is simply 10. Access then finds records that
match that criteria.

The most common type of criteria are called logical expressions. A
logical expression gives a yes or no answer. Access shows you the
record if the answer is yes, but not if the answer is no. The
operators commonly used in logical expressions include <, >, AND,
OR, and NOT.

Although we use uppercase to distinguish operators and functions, case does not matter in the query design grid.

Querying by example

If you want to find all the addresses in Virginia, the criterion for
the state field is simply the following:

Virginia

You may want to add another criterion in the next line (OR) to take
care of different spellings, as follows:

VA

Access puts the text in quotes for you. The result of the query is
all records that have either *Virginia* or *VA* in the state field.

Using operators in criteria expressions

The simplest way to use the query grid is to simply tell Access
what you're looking for by typing a value you want to match in the
Criteria row for the field. But often, your criteria are more complicated than "all records with Virginia in the state field." You use
operators in your criteria expressions to tell Access about more
complex criteria.

This table lists the operators that you're likely to use in a criteria
expression:

Relational Operator	What It Does
=	Finds values equal to text, a number, or date/time
< >	Finds values not equal to text, a number, or date/time

Relational Operator	*What It Does*
<	Finds values less than a given value
<=	Finds values less than or equal to a given value
>	Finds values greater than a given value
>=	Finds values greater than or equal to a given value
BETWEEN	Finds values between or equal to two values
IN	Finds values or text included in a list
LIKE	Finds matches to a pattern

When you type your criteria, you don't have to tell Access that you're looking for Costs<10, for example. When you put <10 in the Criteria row, Access applies the criteria to the field that appears in the Field row of the same column. The following table shows some examples of criteria that use operators:

Expressions with Operator	*What the Operator Tells Access to Do*
<10	Finds record with values less than 10
>10	Finds records with values greater than 10
<>10	Finds records with values not equal to 10
>10 AND <20	Finds records with values between 10 and 20
>=10 AND <=20	Finds records with values between 10 and 20, including 10 and 20
BETWEEN 10 AND 20	The same as >=10 AND <=20
IN ("Virginia", "VA")	Finds the values *Virginia* and *VA*
LIKE "A*"	Finds text beginning with the letter *A*. You can use LIKE with wildcards such as * to tell Access in general terms what you're looking for. For more information on the wildcards that Access recognizes, *see also* "Limiting Data Entries with a Validation Rule," in Part III.

Using AND, OR, and NOT

The most common way to combine expressions that tell Access what you're looking for is to use AND, OR, and NOT in your criteria. These three operators can be a little difficult to figure out unless you aced Logic 101 in college. Here's exactly how they work:

Simple Operator	How It Works in a Query
AND	Tells Access that a particular record must meet more than one criterion to be shown in the datasheet
OR	Tells Access that a particular record must meet only one of several criteria to be shown in the datasheet
NOT	Tells Access that a criterion has to be false for the record to be included in the datasheet

You can combine operators in one criterion expression, such as when you are looking for the following:

```
>10 OR <18 NOT 15
```

This expression produces records with the values 11, 12, 13, 14, 16, and 17 (assuming that all values in the field are integers).

Using multiple criteria

When you have criteria for only one field, you can use the OR operator in two different ways:

✦ Type your expressions into the Criteria row separated by OR.

✦ Type the first expression in the Criteria row, and type subsequent expressions using the Or rows in the query grid.

Whichever approach you take, the result is the same — Access displays records in the datasheet that satisfy one or more of the Criteria expressions.

When you use criteria in multiple fields, Access assumes that you want to find records that meet all the criteria — in other words, that the criteria in each row are considered to be joined by AND statements. If you type criteria on the same row for two fields, a record has to meet both criteria to be displayed on the datasheet.

When you use the Or row, the expressions on each row are treated as though they are joined by AND, but the expressions on different rows are treated as though they are joined by OR. Access first looks at one row of criteria, and finds all the records that meet all the criteria on that row. Then it starts over with the next row of criteria, the Or row, and finds all the records that meet all the criteria on that row. A record only has to meet all the criteria on one row to be displayed in the datasheet.

For example, the following query produces a table including orders placed before November 15 with a total cost of less than $50, and orders placed after November 15 with a total cost over $50.

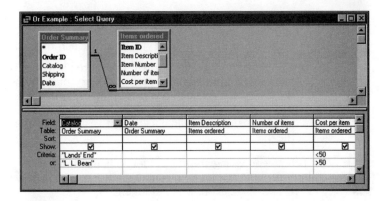

Using dates, times, text, and values in criteria

Access does its best to recognize the types of data that you use in criteria and encloses elements of the expression between the appropriate characters. You are less likely to create criteria that Access doesn't understand, however, if you use those characters yourself.

The following table lists types of elements that you may include in a criteria expression and the character to use to make sure that Access knows that the element is text, a date, a time, a number, or a field name.

Use This Type of Data . . .	In an Expression Like This . . .
Text	"text"
Date	#1-Feb-97#
Time	#12:00am#
Number	10
Field name	[field name]

You can refer to dates or times by using any allowed format. December 25, 1999, 12/25/99, and 25-Dec-99 are all formats that Access recognizes. You can use AM/PM or 24-hour time.

Saving a Query

You don't have to save a query. Often, queries are created on the fly to answer a question. You don't need to clutter your database with queries that you're unlikely to need again.

That said, you can certainly save a query design (but not the query datasheet) when you need to. Use any of the following methods:

✦ In Design or Datasheet view, click the Save button or choose File➪Save. If you haven't saved the query yet, Access asks you for a name for the query. Type the name and then click OK.

 ✦ Close the query (clicking the Close button is a popular method). If you've never saved the query, or if you've changed the query design since you last saved it, Access asks whether you want to save the query. If you've never saved the query, give it a name and then click OK; otherwise, click Yes to save the query.

TIP

I recommend giving your new query a name that tells you what the query does. That way, you won't have to open one query after another to find the one you're looking for.

If you want to create a query similar to one you already have in your database, select or open the query and choose File➪Save As to save the query with a new name. Then you can keep the original query and make changes to the new copy.

Sorting a Query

You can sort a table produced by a query in several ways. The first way is to use the Sort row in the query grid. Use the Sort row to tell Access which field to use to sort the datasheet.

To sort by a field, display your query in Design view and follow these steps:

1. Move the cursor to the Sort row in the column that contains the field according to which you want to sort.

2. Display the drop-down list for the Sort row.

   Access displays the options for sorting: Ascending, Descending, and (not sorted).

3. Choose Ascending or Descending.

You can use the Sort row in the query grid to sort by more than one field. You may want to sort the records in the datasheet by last name, for example, but more than one person may have the same last name. You can specify another field (perhaps first name) as the second sort key. If you want, you can specify more than two fields by which to sort.

When you sort using more than one field, Access always works from left to right, first sorting the records by the first field (the primary sort key) that has Ascending or Descending in the Sort row, and then sorting any records with the same primary sort key value by the second sort key.

You can also sort the datasheet that results from the query, using the same technique you use to sort any datasheet: Click the field that you want to sort by and then click the Sort Ascending or Sort Descending button. *See also* "Sorting Your Data," in Part III.

You cannot sort by a Memo or OLE Data Type field.

Using a Query Wizard

If you click the New button in the Queries tab of the Database window, you see not one but four wizards to help you build your query. The wizard you use depends on what you want your query to do.

The following table lists the four query wizards and tells when you may find each useful.

Query Wizard	When to Use It
Simple Query Wizard	Use this wizard to build a select query. If you want to perform summary calculations with the query, the wizard can help you. If you have criteria, however, you still have to enter them in Design view, so the Simple Query Wizard is not a huge improvement over designing the query yourself. *See also* "Creating a Select Query," in this part, for specifics about using the Simple Query Wizard.
Crosstab Query Wizard	Use this wizard to create a crosstab query. *See also* "Creating a Crosstab Query," in this part, for specific information about using the Crosstab Query Wizard.
Find Duplicates Query Wizard	Use this wizard to find duplicate data in the database.
Find Unmatched Query Wizard	Use this wizard to find records with no corresponding records in related tables.

Wizards give you help creating queries, but the queries that they create are just like the ones you create — you can see them in Design or Datasheet view and do anything with them that you might do with any other query of the same type.

Using a query wizard and studying the Design view of the queries that they create is a good way to learn how to use some of the more advanced features of queries.

Start a query wizard by following these steps:

1. Display the Queries view of the Database window.

2. Click the New button. Access displays the New Query dialog box.

3. Select the wizard you want to use. On the left side of the dialog box, Access displays a brief summary of what the wizard does.

4. Click OK. Access starts the wizard that you chose.

See also "Working with Wizards," in Part I.

Find Duplicates Query Wizard

Use this wizard when you want to find duplicate entries in a field in a table or query. The Find Duplicates Query Wizard can help you find identical records as well as records with the same name and different addresses, for example.

The Find Duplicates Query Wizard needs to know the following things:

✦ The table or query you want it to examine: The wizard displays table names first — if you want to see query names, click the Queries or Both radio button.

✦ The fields in the table or query you picked that may have duplicate information: Select fields that may have duplicate entries and click the right arrow to move them into the Duplicate-Value Fields list box.

✦ Any additional fields that you want to see in the datasheet produced by the query: Seeing additional fields can be useful if you're editing or deleting duplicated records.

✦ The name of the query.

When you click the Finish button and display the datasheet, you see a list of records. Duplicates are listed in groups. You can edit this datasheet to update your data or to delete unneeded records by editing the datasheet, or by using the query design created by the wizard to create an update or delete query.

Find Unmatched Query Wizard

The Find Unmatched Query Wizard finds records in one table that have no matching records in another, related table. You may store orders in one table and details about customers in another table, for example. If the tables are linked by, say, a Customer Number field, the Unmatched Query Wizard can tell you whether you have any customers listed in the Orders table who aren't listed in the Customers table.

The Find Unmatched Query Wizard needs to know the following things:

✦ The table (or query) in which all records should have related records. In the preceding example, this is the Order table where the details of each order are stored. (You should have a related record about each customer.) If you want to choose a query, click the Queries or Both radio button.

✦ The name of the table that contains the related records. In the example, this is the Customer table where the details about each customer are stored. If you want to see queries in addition to tables, click the Queries or Both radio button.

✦ The names of the related fields. Access makes a guess, especially if there is a field in each table with the same name. (It's a little odd that Access can't figure out the names of the related fields by itself, especially if you've defined relationships, but there it is.)

✦ The fields that you want to see in the datasheet resulting from the query.

✦ The name for the query.

Viewing Table Relationships in a Query

Although you can perform a query on unrelated tables, you're likely to get more useful results if the tables are linked. When you put unrelated tables in a query, Access attempts to find a relationship between the tables by comparing the fields in each table. If Access finds two fields that have the same name and the same type of data, it automatically creates a relationship between them.

See also "Relating (Linking) Tables," in Part II, for more information about how to link tables.

You can view the Relationships window by right-clicking the table pane of the query Design view and choosing Relationships from the shortcut menu. When you finish creating or editing relationships, close the Relationships window to return to query Design view. The changes you make in the Relationships window are reflected in the Table pane.

If the relationship lines look all tangled in the Table pane of query Design view, you can move the tables around, just as you can when you view relationships. Just click the title bar of the table and drag it to a new position.

You can create relationships in the query Design view, but the relationship will exist only in the query you defined it in. Generally you'll find it more useful to define all relationships in the Relationships window.

Viewing Top Values

If all you care about is the top values produced by a query, you can tell Access so. Use the Top Values option in the toolbar in query Design view to see the top records produced by the query. A value in the Top Values option shows you that many records in the datasheet; a percentage shows you that percentage of the records that the query found.

Here's what you do to display the top values found by a query:

1. Create your query with all the fields and criteria that you need.

2. Double-check the first sort field, which determines the records that end up at the top of the datasheet.

3. Change the Top Values option by typing a value or a value followed by a percent sign. You can also choose a value from the drop-down list.

4. Click the View button to see only the top values in the datasheet.

Working with Query Datasheets

The result of a query looks a great deal like a table — in fact, it really is a table that you can sort, filter, navigate, and use to enter data. This subset of your data is sometimes called a dynaset. The word dynaset is used because the data that you see in the datasheet is a dynamic subset of your data.

A dynaset is dynamic because the result of a query is updated to reflect changes in the data in your tables. The actual records displayed in a dynaset — the result of a query — are not stored in the database; only the design of the query is stored, and each time you open the query in Datasheet view, it determines which records fit the query criteria.

However, you can edit the data in the query datasheet. Any changes you make are reflected in the table that holds the data you changed.

Because working with queries in Datasheet view is similar to working with tables in Datasheet view, you should turn to Part III for specific instructions on working in the Datasheet view.

See also "Editing Data in a Datasheet," in Part III.

See also "Adding Data to Your Datasheet," in Part III.

See also "Moving Around a Datasheet," in Part III.

See also "Filtering Your Data," in Part III.

See also "Sorting Your Data," in Part III.

See also "Formatting Datasheets," in Part III.

 To return to Query Design view, click the View button.

Part V

Reporting Results

Compiling exactly the data you're looking for is all fine and good, but making that data look great so that you can print it, pass it around, and astound your friends is the whole point, right? In Access 2000, spiffy output comes in the form of reports.

In this part . . .

- ✔ Using the Report Wizard to create awesome reports
- ✔ Creating a report in Report Design view
- ✔ Creating AutoReports
- ✔ Formatting reports
- ✔ Creating sections in your reports to group your data
- ✔ Creating charts with the Chart Wizard
- ✔ Creating labels with the Label Wizard
- ✔ Creating Snapshot reports to send to people who don't have Access

About Reports

Reports are the best way to take information from Access 2000 and put it on paper. In a report, you can choose the size and format in which to display your data. You can even add pictures and graphs to your reports.

Reports can group information from different tables — for instance, you can display the customer information just once, and list all the items the customer has ordered. You can also use calculations in reports to create totals, subtotals, and other results. You can create invoices with reports, as well as other output that summarizes your data. Thanks to the trusty Label Wizard, reports are also the best way to create mailing labels from the data contained in a database.

You can create a report from one table or query, or from several linked tables and queries. You can even create a report from a filtered table.

Adding a New Report to Your Database

The best way to create any report is to start with the Report Wizard — especially if you want to create a report that groups data using one or more fields. Chances are, the Report Wizard knows more about designing multilevel reports than you do, and when the Wizard finishes, you can take over and add distinctive formatting touches in Design view.

See also "Creating a Report with the Report Wizard," in this part.

See also "Adding a Report Created in Design View," in this part.

See also "Creating Sections in a Report," in this part.

You create a report the same way that you create other objects in your database. Follow these steps:

1. Display the Reports view in the Database window.

2. Click the <u>N</u>ew button. Access displays the New Report dialog box, giving you many choices for creating a new report.

Icons for the two most popular methods of creating a new report are displayed in the Reports section of the Database window: Create Report in Design View and Create Report By Using Wizard. Double-click either of these icons to create a report using the method in the icon name.

The following table describes the choices on the New Report dialog box and tells you when to use each of them.

Option in New Report Dialog Box	When to Use It
Design View	When you want to design your own report from scratch in Report Design view. *See also* "Adding a Report Created in Design View," in this part.
Report Wizard	When you want Access to create a report, using the fields, grouping, and sorting that you provide. *See also* "Creating a Report with the Report Wizard," in this part.
AutoReport: Columnar	When you want to create a report from one table or query and arrange data from each record on a separate page, with field names in a column on the left and the data for the field in a column on the right. *See also* "Adding an AutoReport to Your Database," in this part.
AutoReport: Tabular	When you want to create a report from one table or query and arrange the data in a table, with field names at the top of columns and data from each record displayed as a row in the table (as in a datasheet). *See also* "Adding an AutoReport to Your Database," in this part.
Chart Wizard	When you want to create a chart from data stored in one table or query. *See also* "Creating Charts with the Chart Wizard," in this part.
Label Wizard	When you want to put data from one table or query on labels. *See also* "Creating Labels with the Label Wizard," in this part.

Adding an AutoReport to Your Database

AutoReports are an easy way to create a report out of one table or query. AutoReports don't have the flexibility that regular reports have — you can't create groups with an AutoReport, for example — but they are an excellent way to get your data into a report quickly. You can customize an AutoReport by using the formatting tricks described elsewhere in this part. *See also* "Formatting Reports with AutoFormat" and "Changing Font and Font Size," both in this part.

Access has two kinds of AutoReports: columnar and tabular. A columnar AutoReport prints the field names in a column on the left and the data for the record in a column on the right.

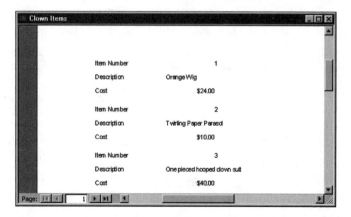

A tabular AutoReport looks similar to a datasheet. Data is displayed in columns with field names as the column headers.

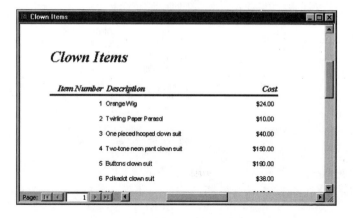

To create a columnar AutoReport, follow these steps:

1. In the Database window, select the table or query that contains the data you want to display in a report.

2. Click the arrow next to the New Object button and choose AutoReport from the drop-down list. Access creates the report.

Another way to create an AutoReport — and the only way to create a tabular AutoReport — is to click the New button in the Reports tab of the Database window. Access displays the New Report dialog box — choose the type of AutoReport and the table or query that you want it to use; then click OK. Access creates the report.

Adding a Report with the Report Wizard

Using the Report Wizard is the best way to create a report. You may be happy with the resulting report, or you may want to edit the report further, but if you use the Report Wizard, at least you have a report to work with.

One big advantage of using the Report Wizard is that you can choose fields for the report from more than one table or query — you don't have to gather all the data you want in the report into one table or query.

See also "Working with Wizards," in Part I.

The Report Wizard displays different windows depending on the data and options you select, so don't be surprised if you don't see every window of the wizard. Follow these steps to create a report with the Report Wizard:

1. Display the Reports view in the Database window and double-click the Create Report by Using Wizard icon.

Access displays the first Report Wizard window, where you select the fields that you want to use in your report.

You can also start the wizard by displaying the New Report dialog box (click the New button or choose Report from the New Object button drop-down list), selecting Report Wizard, and clicking OK.

2. From the Tables/Queries list, select the first table or query from which you want to select fields.

3. Add the fields you want displayed in the report to the Selected Fields list.

4. Repeat Steps 3 and 4 for fields in other tables or queries until all the fields you want to display in the report appear in the Selected Fields list.

5. Click the Next button to see the next window of the wizard. If the fields you've chosen for your reports are grouped in some way (usually by a many-to-one relationship with another field chosen for the report) you will see this window, which allows you to choose which table you want to use to group your data.

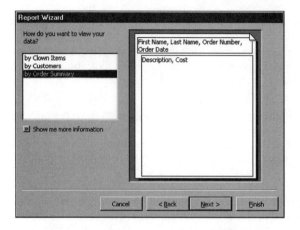

Double-click a table name to group the data in the report by using that table; then click <u>N</u>ext to continue to the next window, which lets you group by individual fields.

6. Add grouping fields if desired by selecting the field and clicking the right-arrow button (>).

You can change the importance of a field in the grouping hierarchy by selecting the field on the right side of the window and then clicking the up- and down-arrow buttons labeled Priority.

Click the Grouping Options button to display the Grouping Intervals dialog box, where you can specify exactly how to group records using the fields you chose as grouping fields.

The Grouping Intervals dialog box lets you select grouping intervals for each field used to group the report — different data types have different grouping-interval options:

If You Group by a Field Containing This	You Can Group by This Interval
Date	Day, month, year, and so on
Number	In 10s, 50s, 100s, 500s, 1,000s, 5,000s, and 10,000s so that you can categorize values by magnitude
Text	Using up to five initial letters
All types of data	The Normal option groups by using the entire field (Only records that have exactly the same value are grouped together.)

Click OK to leave the Grouping Intervals dialog box.

7. When you finish grouping your data, click the Next button to see options for sorting and summarizing. Access automatically sorts the report by the first grouping field.

This window allows you to tell Access how you want to sort the detail section of the report. The detail section is the part of the report that displays the records within each group. You don't have to change anything in this window if you don't need the detail section sorted in any particular order.

If you want to specify a sort order for the detail objects, display the drop-down list of field names next to the box labeled "1." Click the Sort button to change the sort order from ascending (A to Z, 1 to 10) to descending (Z to A, 10 to 1). Click the button again to change the sort order back. You can sort by up to four fields — use the additional boxes to specify additional fields on which to sort. Additional sort fields are used only when the initial sort field is identical for two or more records — then the next sort field is used to determine in what order to display those records.

8. To display summary calculations, click the Summary Options button. Access displays the Summary Options dialog box where you can tell Access to display totals or other calculated summary data in the report. The options displayed in the Summary Options dialog box depend on the data in your report.

9. Click check boxes to indicate the field(s) you want to summarize and what kind of calculation you want for the summary.

This dialog box also has options that allow you to show the Summary Only or the Detail and Summary data. If you choose Summary Only, the report displays only the result of the calculation, not the data from the records that were used to calculate the result. If you want to see the data in individual records, choose Detail and Summary data.

Also on this dialog box also is a check box to tell Access to Calculate percent of Total for Sums; Access then calculates the percentage of the total that each group represents.

10. When you're done with the Summary Options dialog box, click OK; you see the window with sorting options again. Then click Next in the Report Wizard window to view the next window. Access displays the window that allows you to specify how to lay out your report.

11. Choose the layout that you prefer and the orientation that works best with your report. You can preview the layout options by clicking one of the Layout radio buttons. The example box on the left changes to show you what your chosen layout looks like.

12. Click Next to see the next window, where you choose the style that you prefer. Styles consist of background shadings, fonts, font sizes, and the other formatting used for your report.

13. Select a style. You can preview each style by clicking it.

14. Click the Next button to view the last window of the wizard.

15. Type a new name for the report (if you don't like the name that the Report Wizard has chosen). If you want to view the report in Design view, click Modify the Report's Design; otherwise, the Preview the Report radio button is selected, and Access shows you the report in Print Preview. You can also tell Access that you want to see the Help window (which gives you hints on how to customize the report) by clicking the check box titled Display Help on Working with the Report?

16. Click the Finish button to view your report. Your computer may whir and grind for a minute before your report appears.

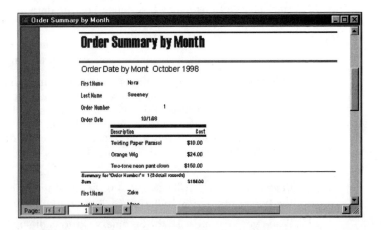

Although the Report Wizard does well setting up groups, it doesn't create a perfect report. Some controls may be the wrong size, and the explanatory text the wizard uses for calculated fields is a little pedantic. Display the report in Design view to fix anything that's wrong with it. *See also* "Changing the Size of an Object," "Editing Objects in a Report," and "Moving an Object," all in this part.

Adding a Report Created in Design View

You may have a personal thing against wizards, or you may just need to know how to create or edit a report in Design View. Whichever is the case, this section covers how to add *controls* that tell Access what to display on the report.

Controls tell Access what you want to see on your report: Text, the contents of a field, and lines are all added to reports by using controls. I tell you how to add specific controls to your report later in this section. Follow these general steps to create the report itself:

1. Display Reports in the Database window by clicking the Reports button in the Objects list.

2. Click the New button. Access displays the New Report dialog box.

3. Select Design View (it is probably already selected).

4. Select the query or table on which you want to base the report from the drop-down list at the bottom of the dialog box. If you want to bind the report to more than one table, the easiest way is to create a query that includes all the fields you want to display in the report.

Binding a report to a query can be very useful — it means that you can create criteria for choosing the records that appear in your report so that Access doesn't include them all. You may want to make a report that includes only clients whose payments are overdue, for example, or you may want a report that includes only the addresses of people whom you're inviting to your wedding.

5. Click OK.

Access displays the Report Design view.

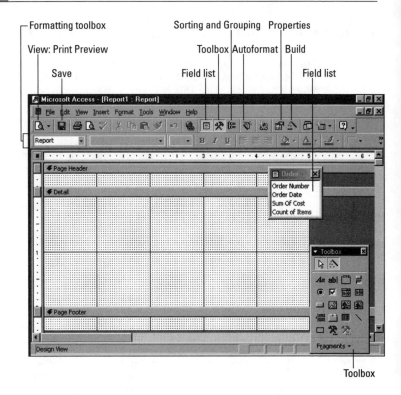

Formatting toolbox

View: Print Preview

Save

Sorting and Grouping Properties

Toolbox Autoformat Build

Field list

Field list

Toolbox

6. Save the report design by clicking the Save button on the toolbar. Give the report a name that will help you and others figure out which data it displays.

Remember to save your report design often.

After you've created the blank report, you're ready to start adding controls to it, as explained later in this section.

Although it seems like it would be easy to create a report in Design view by double-clicking the Create Report in Design View icon, this method does not allow you to select the table or query you want to base the report on. If you create a report this way, you have to select the table or query that has the data in the Record Source option on the report Properties dialog box.

See also "Adding Calculations to a Report," "Creating Sections in a Report," "Changing Page Layout," and "Changing Font and Font Size," in this part for more information on how to make your report look the way you want it to.

For an in-depth discussion on how to design reports so that they do what you want them to do, see *Access 2000 For Windows For Dummies,* or *Access For Windows 95 Bible* (both published by IDG Books Worldwide, Inc.).

Using tools in Report Design view

Creating reports is complicated enough that Access gives you a group of new tools to work with in report Design view: the buttons and boxes in the Formatting toolbar and in the Toolbox. Access also displays the grid in the background (to help you align objects in the report), as well as the rulers at the top and left of the design window.

You can choose which of these tools you want to appear by using the View menu when you're in Design view. Items with a check mark appear in the design window

You can also display and close the Toolbox by clicking the Toolbox button on the toolbar.

Each type of object that you may want to add to your report has a different button in the Toolbox — choose the type of object that you want and then click the spot in the report where you want to put the object.

You can move the Toolbox so that it appears along one edge of the Access window instead of floating free. To anchor the Toolbox to an edge, click its title bar and drag the Toolbox to one edge of the screen. A gray outline shows you where the Toolbox will be when you drop it. When the gray outline appears in one row or column against one side of the Access window, release the mouse. You can make the Toolbox free-floating again by clicking and dragging by

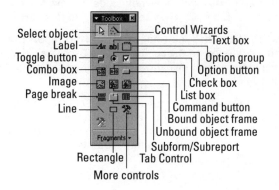

the top (if the Toolbox is vertical) or the left of the bar. (In fact, you can perform this trick with any toolbar.)

You can also make the Toolbox a different size by clicking and dragging a border. The size you choose affects the number of buttons that appear on each row.

You can control which buttons appear in the Toolbox by clicking the down arrow on the Toolbox title bar and choosing Add or Remove Buttons. You see a list of buttons with check marks next to them. Buttons with check marks appear in the Toolbox; those without do not. Click a button name to add or remove the check mark.

Adding a control

A report is made up of controls that tell Access what to display on the report. To display the contents of a field in a report, you have to create a *bound* control. The control is bound to a field, which tells Access to display the contents of a field in that control.

The people who developed Access knew you would want to add fields to reports frequently. So they made it possible to add a field to a report with a single drag-and-drop procedure, rather than forcing you to use two steps — first creating the control and then telling Access to display the contents of a field in the control.

To add a control that displays the contents of a field to a report, display the report in Design view and follow these steps:

1. Display the Field List window by clicking the Field List button on the toolbar. Access displays a small window that contains the names of the fields available to use on the report. If you didn't bind a table or query to the report in the New Report dialog box, you won't have any fields to view. *See also* "Binding a Table or Query to a Report," in this part.

2. Drag the field that you want to use in your report from the field list window to the report design. Drop the field in the place in the report design where you want the contents of the field to appear.

Access puts a field control and a label control in the report. The label control contains the name of the field, followed by a colon. The field control tells Access to display the contents of the field. You can edit or delete either control. *See also* "Editing Objects in a Report," later in this part.

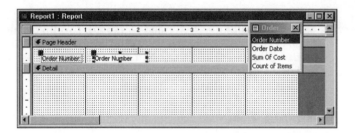

You can put several fields in the report by Ctrl+clicking to select multiple field names. You can also select consecutive fields by clicking the first field and then Shift+clicking the last field that you want to select. Then drag all the selected fields to the design grid where they appear one under the other. Once in the design grid, you can edit and move the controls. *See also* "Moving a Control," in this part

If you want to get rid of the label that Access adds automatically, or move the label to a different place in the report, select the label and then press Ctrl+X. To display the label in a different position, click the report design where you want the label to appear and then press Ctrl+V. You can move the label by dragging the larger handle that appears on it's upper left corner when you select it.

See also "Selecting Parts of a Report," later in this part.

Adding a line

Remember that what you see in Report Design view is not exactly how the printed report will appear. Not everything you see in Design view prints — for example, those little dots and the vertical and horizontal lines you see in the background of the Design view, as well as the boxes around the objects you put in the report design, are all non-printing elements of the design. To see what the printed report will look like, click the Print Preview button or the View button.

You can put a vertical, horizontal, or diagonal line into a report by adding it to the report design. If you want to create a box to surround an object, you actually want to work with the object's border. *See also* "Playing with Borders," later in this part.

Insert a line into a report by clicking the Line button in the Toolbox. Then move the mouse pointer into the report design, click where you want the line to begin, and drag to where you want the line to end. A line must begin and end in the same section of the report.

After you create a line, you can change its color and width by using the Line/Border Color and Line/Border Width buttons in the Formatting toolbar. You can delete the line by selecting it and pressing the Delete (Del) key. You can move the line by clicking it and dragging it to a new position or by using the Cut and Paste buttons on the toolbar.

Adding a label

If you want to create a text label that isn't attached to a field control, you can do so by using the Label button in the Toolbox. For example, you may want to create a label to display the name of the report.

Display the report in Design view and follow these steps to add a label to the report:

 1. Click the Label button in the Toolbox.

2. Click and drag in the report design to create a box the right size and position for your label.

3. Type the text that you want to appear in the label.

4. Press Enter.

 If you want more than one line of text in your label box, press Ctrl+Enter to start a new line.

To edit the label, click the text box once to select it; then press F2 to edit the label. Press Enter when the edits are complete, or Esc to cancel the edits you made.

Adding pictures and other objects

You can add a picture to a report in several ways; the method you use depends on how you want to use the picture. A picture can be bound or unbound (in fact, any object on the report can be bound or unbound). An *unbound* object is always the same, such as a logo. A *bound* object is tied to one or more fields and will change for different records. You may store a picture of each person in your address database, for example, and display the appropriate pictures next to the addresses in your report using a bound object. Or you may display your logo on each invoice using an unbound object.

You can link or insert a picture. A *linked* picture is stored in its own file; Access goes out and finds it when necessary. The contents of the linked file may change — Access will simply display the current contents. An *inserted* picture is stored in the Access database.

You can display a picture as an object in the report, or you can display it in the background of the report, like a watermark. If the picture is an object in the report, you can edit the picture by double-clicking it.

The easiest way to insert a picture into a report is to follow these steps:

1. Display the report in Design view.

 2. Click the Image button in the toolbox.

3. Click the report where you want the picture to appear. Access displays the Insert Picture dialog box, where you can find the file that contains the picture you want to display on the report.

4. In the Insert Picture dialog box, navigate your folders until you find the file that you need.

5. Select the file and then click OK.

 You can even search the Web for an appropriate picture; just click the Search the Web button in the Insert Picture dialog box to launch Internet Explorer.

To find out more about using Internet Explorer to search the Web, see *Internet Explorer For Windows For Dummies,* by Doug Lowe (published by IDG Books Worldwide, Inc.).

You can change the size and position of a picture the same way that you change the size or position of any object in the report. *See also* "Moving an Object" and "Changing the Size of an Object" both in this part.

To link to a picture, follow these steps:

1. Insert the picture using the previous set of steps.

2. Select the picture object in the report.

3. Display the properties of the image by clicking the Properties button on the toolbar.

4. Change the Picture Type to Linked (use the drop-down list to see the options). The Picture Type option is in the Format and All tabs of the Image Properties dialog box.

You can delete a picture from the report by selecting it and pressing the Delete key.

Adding Calculations to a Report

See also "Calculating Fields," in Part IV.

To include calculated fields in a report, you must put the expression for the calculation in a text box in the Report design view. The first step in adding a calculation is to create a text box in your report. The section of the report that you put the calculation depends on the type of result you want — is this a calculation for each record (such as multiplying the cost by the number of items ordered) or for the group of records (such as adding the cost of each item to calculate the cost of the order)?

You often use calculations to summarize the data in one section or in an entire report. The place to put those summary calculations is in the section footer or report footer. *See also* "Creating Sections in a Report" in this part.

To create a text box, follow these steps:

1. Display the report in Design view.

   See also "Previewing Your Report" and "Creating a Report Using Design View," later in this part.

 2. Click the Text Box button in the Toolbox. If you don't see the Toolbox, click the Toolbox button on the toolbar.

3. Click and drag to create a box in the place where you want to display the calculation result. Make the text box the right size to display the result of the expression.

   The report must be bound to a table or query before you can create a text box — the "Record Source" appears in the report properties dialog box. *See also* "Binding a Table to a Report," in this part.

4. Click inside the box to display the cursor.

5. Type an equal sign (=) to begin the expression.

6. Type the expression that you want Access to calculate. You may want to display the expression in a Zoom box by pressing Ctrl+F2 so that you can see the whole thing.

   See also "Calculating Fields (Building Expressions)," in Part IV.

 If you want to use the Expression Builder to create an expression, you need to display the properties for the text box. Select the text box and then click the Properties button on the toolbar.

See also "Selecting Parts of a Report" in this part.

The expression appears in the Control Source box on the Data tab. To use the Expression Builder, click the Control Source box and then click the Build button that appears to the right of the option. *See also* "Calculating Fields: Using the Expression Builder," in Part IV.

 You may find the Running Sum property useful. If you choose Yes for this option, Access creates a running sum — that is, it adds each section's total to the total calculated for the section(s) that appears before it in the report.

Adding Color to a Report

The Formatting toolbar provides options for adding color to a report. You can change the color of text, backgrounds, and lines by using one of three buttons on the Formatting toolbar. The following table lists the buttons on the toolbar that control color, what they're called, and how they work:

Button	What It's Called	What It Does
	Fill/Back Color	Changes the color of the background of the selected object or the background of the selected section when no control is selected.
	Font/Fore Color	Changes the color of the text in the selected object.
	Line/Border Color	Changes the color of the border (the box around the object) of the selected object; also changes the color of a selected line.

You use each of these buttons the same way. Follow these steps:

1. Select the object that you want to work with.

2. Click the arrow to the right of the button that changes colors. Access displays a palette of colors.

3. Click the color that you want to use.

 If you want the object to be invisible or the same color as the general background, choose Transparent from the top of the color grid.

Adding Dates and Page Numbers

Access 2000 is a whiz at many things, including adding dates and page numbers. Access can number the pages of your report or put today's date in a report — all you have to do is ask.

The most sensible place to add the date and page number is in the page header or page footer of the report. The Report Wizard puts both the date and the page number (in the format *Page X of Y*) in the page footer for you.

Inserting the date and/or time

If you want to add the date and/or time yourself, rather than relying on the Report Wizard, display the report in Design view and follow these steps:

1. Click the section (or *band*) in which you want the date and/or time to appear. *See also* "Creating Sections in a Report."

2. Choose Insert⇨Date and Time to insert the date, the time, or both. The Date and Time dialog box appears. The Date and Time dialog box provides options for including the date, the time, or both, and allows you to choose the format.

3. Select Include Date and/or Include Time and then select the format you want. Check the Sample box to see how the date and/or time will appear on your report.

4. Click OK. Access adds the date and/or time to the section of your report that you selected in Step 1.

You can move and format the date and time controls just as you do any other. *See also* "Moving an Object," "Changing Font and Font Size," and "Changing the Size of an Object," all in this part.

Inserting page numbers

To add page numbers yourself, rather than relying on the Report Wizard, display the report in Design view and follow these steps:

1. Choose Insert⇨Page Numbers. The Page Numbers dialog box appears. The Page Numbers dialog box gives you several choices about how your page numbers will appear on your report:

• **Format:** Select Page N to show only the current page number, or select Page N of M to show both the current page number and the total number of pages.

• **Position:** Decide whether the page numbers will appear in the page header or the page footer.

• **Alignment:** Click the down-arrow of this list box and choose Center (centers page numbers between the margins), Left (aligns page numbers with the left margin), Right (aligns page numbers with the right margin), Inside (prints page numbers alternately on the right and left sides of facing pages), or Outside (prints page numbers alternately on the left and right sides of facing pages).

- **Show Number on First Page:** Deselect (remove the check mark from) this option if you want to hide the page number on the first page of your report (a good way to keep your title page spiffy).

2. Change the options in the dialog box to suit your purposes.

3. Click OK. Access puts the page number in the position you selected (Top of Page or Bottom of Page).

You can move and format the page number control just as you do any other. *See also* "Moving an Object," "Changing Font and Font Size," and "Changing the Size of an Object," all in this part.

Aligning Report Objects

Access automatically aligns the contents of a bound control — that is, a control that displays the contents of a field: text is left justified and numbers and dates are right justified within the control. The three alignment buttons on the Formatting toolbar allow you to customize the alignment of the contents of a control.

To change the alignment of the contents of a control, follow these steps:

1. Select the object.

2. Click the appropriate alignment button: Align Left, Center, or Align Right.

Align Left

Align Right

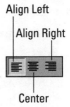

Center

See also "Moving an Object," for information on aligning controls (rather than the contents of the control).

Binding a Table or Query to a Report

In order to use fields from a table or query in a report design, you must first bind the table or query to the report using the Report Properties. Follow these steps:

1. Display the Report Properties by right-clicking report selector in the top-left corner of the report (***see also*** "Selecting Parts of a Report," in this part) and choosing <u>P</u>roperties.

2. Click the Data tab.

3. Click the drop-down list for Record Source, the first property displayed. Choose the table or query you want to bind to the report.

4. Click the Close button (X) to close the Properties sheet.

Now you can display a list of fields in the bound report or query by clicking the Field List button on the toolbar. ***See also*** "Adding a Field Control," in this part.

Changing Date or Number Formats

To change the format of a date or number in a field control, you need to use the Format property for the control. Follow these steps to display the properties for the control and change the format:

1. Select the control.

2. Display the control's properties by clicking the Properties button.

3. Click the Format option (in the All and the Format tabs).

4. Choose the format that you want to use from the drop-down list.

5. Close the Properties box.

Changing Font and Font Size

Changing the font and font size of text in a report is one of the easiest formatting tasks. All you need to do is select the control that contains the text you want to format and choose the font and/ or font size you want from the Font and Font Size options on the formatting toolbar.

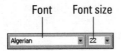

Font   Font size

You can make the text bold, italic, and/or underlined by clicking the Bold, Italic, and/or Underline button(s) while the object is selected.

TIP If you choose a font that makes the text too large to fit in the control, make the control larger. *See also* "Changing the Size of an Object" in this part.

Changing Formatting According to Content (Conditional Formatting)

Access allows you to change some text attributes (bold, italic, underlined, fill/back color, font color, special effects) of a control in a report or form based on the control's content. To use conditional formatting, follow these steps:

1. Select the control in Design view.

2. Choose Format⇨Conditional Formatting from the menu to display the Conditional Formatting dialog box.

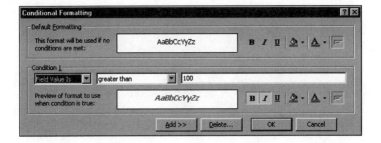

3. If desired, use the buttons in the default Formatting section of the dialog box to change the Default Formatting — this is the format that will be used if no conditions are met.

4. Define the first condition for the contents of the field for the alternate format. Use the first row of options in the Condition 1 section of the dialog box.

5. Select the format for control when the condition is met.

6. If you need to add conditions, click the Add button to display additional Condition sections on the dialog box. Repeat Steps 4 and 5 for the other conditions.

7. Click OK to close the dialog box.

8. View the Report Preview to see if your formatting is appearing as you want it.

To edit conditional formatting, select the control and choose Format⇨Conditional Formatting menu to display the Conditional Formatting dialog box. If you delete any values from the condition (for example, I would delete *100* in the figure), you delete the condition.

Changing Page Layout

Use the Page Setup dialog box to change the way Access prints your report on the page. Display the Page Setup dialog box by choosing File⇨Page Setup when working with the report in either Design view or Print Preview.

Choosing landscape versus portrait

To choose whether the report should appear in *landscape* (longer than it is tall) or *portrait* (taller than it is long) orientation, follow these steps:

1. Display the Page Setup dialog box by choosing File⇨Page Setup.

2. Click the Page tab at the top of the dialog box.

3. Select the Portrait or Landscape radio button.

4. Click OK to close the dialog box.

Adjusting margins

To change the margins for a report, follow these steps:

1. Display the Page Setup dialog box by choosing File⇨Page Setup.

2. Click the Margins tab at the top of the dialog box.

3. Change the Top, Bottom, Left, and Right margins as necessary.

4. Click OK to close the dialog box.

See also "Changing Margins," in Part VII.

Printing in columns

If your report takes up less than half the width of a page, you can tell Access to print it in multiple columns. The options for columns are in the Page Setup dialog box.

To create columns in your report, follow these steps:

1. Display the Page Setup dialog box by choosing File⇨Page Setup.

2. Click the Columns tab to view options for columns.

3. Use the Number of Columns setting to tell Access how many columns you want on each page.

4. Use the Column Layout settings to tell Access the order in which it should print on the page. Access can work across a row before starting a new row (Across, Then Down) or work down a column before starting the next column (Down, Then Across).

5. Click OK to close the dialog box.

If you tell Access to use more columns than will fit on the page, you get an error message. Try using fewer columns, or try using landscape orientation. (Orientation options appear on the Page tab of the Page Setup dialog box.) If the columns fit, Access rearranges the print preview of the report; look at it and see whether you like what you've done.

You may want to use the other options in the Columns tab of the Page Setup dialog box, which I describe in the following table:

Option	What It Does
Row Spacing	Tells Access how much space (in inches) to leave between rows. (A row is one record's worth of data.)
Column Spacing	Tells Access how much space (in inches) to leave between columns.
Width	Specifies the width of the column. (Access sets this option automatically; if you make the width smaller, the data may not fit in the column.)
Height	Specifies the height of a row. (Access sets this option automatically.)
Same As Detail	Tells Access to size the column to fit the Detail section of the report when a check appears in the check box.

Changing the Size of an Object

You can change the size of a control by clicking and dragging the border of the control while you're in Design view. Follow these steps:

1. Select the object whose size you want to change. Anchors (little black boxes) appear around the selected object.

   See also "Selecting Parts of a Report," in this part.

2. Move the mouse pointer to one of the anchors. The pointer turns into a two-headed arrow, indicating that you can change the size of the box.

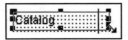

3. Drag the edge of the box so that the object is the size you want it to be.

The Format⇨Size menu has additional options that allow you to change the size of an object:

✦ If you just want an object to be just the right size to display its contents, choose Format⇨Size⇨To Fit.

✦ If you want several objects to be the same size, select all the objects and then choose Format⇨Size⇨To Tallest, To Shortest, To Widest, or To Narrowest. Access makes all the objects the same size. If you choose To Shortest, for example, Access changes all the objects to the same size as the shortest object that was selected when you chose the menu option.

Charting with the Chart Wizard

If you want to create charts in Access, the Chart Wizard is a good way to get started.

See also "Working with Wizards," in Part I.

You may want to add a chart to an existing report, or create a chart that stands alone. The Chart Wizard allows you to do either of these, but you need to start the Chart Wizard differently depending on the option you choose:

✦ To include a chart in an existing report, open the report in design view and choose Insert⇨Chart. Click the section of the report where you want the chart to appear to start the Chart

Wizard. The first window of the wizard asks you to select the table or query that contains the fields you want to display in your chart (this window is not displayed when you use the next method to start the Chart Wizard).

✦ To create a chart that is the whole report, display the Reports view of the Database window and click the <u>N</u>ew button. In the New Report dialog box, select Chart Wizard, choose the table or query that contains the data you want to chart, and then click the OK button to start the wizard.

After you've started the wizard and chosen the table or query to bind to the chart, follow these steps to create a chart:

1. Choose the fields you want to chart, and then click Next to see the next window.

If you are charting values by date, make sure that you include the field that contains the date value. For example, if you want to chart calls per week for each week of the year, you need to choose both the field that contains the number of calls data and the field that contains the information about when the calls were received.

2. Select the type of chart that you want to create, and then click <u>N</u>ext to see the next window. When you select a chart type, the wizard gives you some information about the chart type and the kind of data that makes an effective chart of that type.

3. Drag fields onto the chart and tell the wizard how to use the fields you've selected in the chart. This window is a little tricky — trial and error may be your best bet. When you finish, click <u>N</u>ext to see the next window.

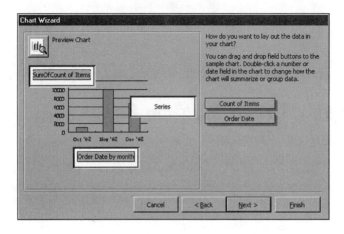

The chart shows three labels: the X-axis (horizontal) label (Date by Month), the Y-axis (vertical) label (SumOfTotal Cost for Items), and the series that are displayed in the chart (which will appear as a legend in the chart).

Double-click a box on the left side of the window to see more detail. When you double-click Order Date by Month, for example, you see a dialog box that allows you to change the grouping shown in the chart to years, quarters, days, and so on. If you double-click SumOfCount of Items, you see a dialog box that allows you to change the calculation from sum to one of the other aggregate functions.

The fields that you've chosen are buttons on the right side of the window; drag them to the chart on the left side to use them as labels or series in thechart. If Access used the wrong fields in any of the labels, you can drag the field name from the left side of the chart to the right side.

4. Give the chart a name, tell Access whether you want to see a legend in the chart (the part of the chart that labels the fields used), and specify whether you want to see the chart in Print Preview or Design view

5. Click Finish to see what you've created.

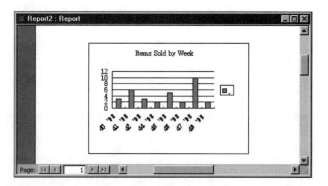

Copying Formatting from One Control to Another

After you go to the effort of prettifying one control, why reinvent the wheel to make another control match it? You can simply copy the formatting from one control to another by using the Format Painter. The Format Painter copies all formatting — colors, fonts, font sizes, border sizes, border styles, and anything else that you can think of.

Follow these steps to copy formatting from one control to another.

1. Select the object that has the formatting you want to copy.

2. Click the Format Painter button on the toolbar. If you want to format more than one object, double-click the Format Painter button. The Format Painter button now looks pushed in. When the mouse pointer is on an object that can be formatted, the pointer has a paintbrush attached to it. When the mouse pointer is on a part of the report that can't be formatted with the Format Painter, the paintbrush has a circle and line over it to indicate that you cannot format there.

3. Click the object to which you want to copy the formatting. Access copies the formatting. If you used a single click to turn the Format Painter on, the mouse pointer loses its paintbrush. If you double-clicked to turn the Format Painter on, you can click additional objects to format them, too. To turn the Format Painter off, click the Format Painter button.

Creating a Report from a Filtered Table

You can filter a table or record and create a report from the resulting records. When the data resulting from the filter changes, the report changes to match.

Here's how to do it:

1. Filter the table and display the filtered records in Datasheet view.

2. Click the arrow to the right of the New Object button and then choose AutoReport or Report from the drop-down list. If you choose AutoReport, Access immediately displays a columnar AutoReport. If you choose Report, Access displays the New Report dialog box.

3. Pick the method you want to use to create the report, and design the report or have a wizard design it for you.

The filter you use is transferred to the report. Changing the filter on the table that you used initially has no effect on the report.

Creating Labels with the Label Wizard

If you need to print your data on labels, the Label Wizard is a great way to get what you need in the right format.

Before you launch the Label Wizard, you need to gather data for the labels into one table or query. You may also want to have your labels on hand, unless you know by heart the Avery number or the exact dimensions.

After you get your data together in one table or query and determine the size or Avery number of your labels, you're ready to run the Label Wizard and let it make your labels.

See also "Working with Wizards," in Part I.

Follow these steps to let the Label Wizard help you make labels:

1. Display the New Report dialog box by clicking the New button in the Reports view of the Database window.

2. Select Label Wizard, and choose the table or query that contains the data for the labels; then click OK to start the wizard. Access displays the window where you tell it about the labels that you're using.

3. Select the manufacturer of your label from the Filter by Manufacturer drop-down list.

If you need to create a new label definition, click the Customize button to open the New Label Size dialog box. Create a new label definition by clicking the New button. Access displays the New Label dialog box. Type a name and select a unit of measure, label type, and orientation. Next, define the labels by filling in the measurements on the sample label page at the bottom of the dialog box. You need to know the dimensions of the labels and the distance between labels. You also need to specify margins on the labels — that is, the distance between the edge of each label and the data on the label.

After you define the label, click OK on the New Label Size or the Edit Label dialog box, and then click the Close button on the New Label Size dialog box to return to the first window of the wizard.

Select the custom label definition you just created. (Make sure the Show custom Label Sizes check box is selected to display custom labels.)

4. Click the Next button to see the next window of the wizard. Choose Text Appearance for the label by specifying the Font name, Font size, Font weight, and Text color for the labels. You can also choose Italic and/or Underline text styles. The format you choose applies to the entire label; you can't format each field separately.

5. Click the Next button. Specify the fields that you want to use in the label.

Put a field in the Prototype Label box by double-clicking it (or by selecting it and then clicking the right-arrow button). Unlike the other wizards that you use, this wizard does not require each field to appear on a separate line; the fields should appear in the Prototype Label list box the same way that you want them to appear in the label.

6. Press Enter or ↓ to move to a new row in the Prototype Label box; otherwise, all the field names will be in the same line. You can add punctuation or additional characters by typing the character(s) you want to appear.

If you are creating address labels, for example, the Prototype label window will probably end up looking something like the one shown in the following figure. Notice the spaces and comma that I typed in.

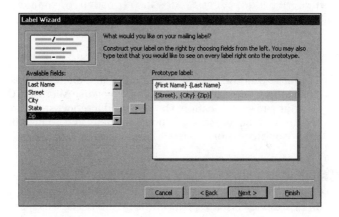

7. Click the Next button to see the next window, which allows you to choose fields on which to sort. Select the field by which you want Access to sort the labels. You can select multiple fields on which to sort, if you want to — the primary sort field is the first listed.

8. Click Next to see the final window of the wizard. Give the report a name (or accept the one that Access suggests).

9. Choose either See the Labels as they Will Look Printed (which displays the report in Print Preview) or Modify the Label Design (which displays the Report Design view) by selecting one of the radio buttons. You may also want to use the Display Help on Working with Labels check box to display a Help window as well as the Design view or Print Preview of your labels.

10. Click Finish to tell the Label Wizard to make your labels.

After you close the wizard, you have to make any additional changes in Report Design view — you cannot edit the labels using the Label Wizard.

Creating a Snapshot Report

The Access Snapshot feature allows you to create static data in electronic form for distribution that can be opened without a full Microsoft Access license. A snapshot file is saved in a .snp file. It contains the contents and format of the Access report. In order to open a snapshot file, you need the Snapshot Viewer (Version 8 or 9). Anyone with Access 2000 installed has the Snapshot Viewer. The Snapshot Viewer is available for download for people without Access 2000 from the Web at the following address:

www.microsoft.com/accessdev/prodinfo/snapshot.htm

You can create a report snapshot by using the Save As/Export command on the File menu.

To create a snapshot file, select the name of the report in the Database window. Choose File⇨Export, and choose Snapshot Format (*.snp) as the Save As Type. If you use Microsoft Outlook as your e-mail application, you can send a report snapshot in an electronic mail message by choosing File⇨Send To in either Microsoft Access or Snapshot Viewer.

Creating Sections in a Report

In Design view, your report is broken into parts, which are called *sections* or *bands*. Sections come in pairs around the Detail section of the report, which is the meat of the report sandwich.

Adding additional sections to a report allows you to group data using a particular field — if you have a number of records with the same value in a field, you can display those records together on the report. For example, if you have a file that stores the date of a transaction, you can create a Date section and then group records that have the same date.

For more information about grouping data in reports, see *Access 2000 For Windows For Dummies*, by John Kaufeld. If you're into the heavy-duty details of creating reports, check out *Access For Windows 2000 Bible,* by Cary Prague and Michael Irwin. (Both books are, of course, published by IDG Books Worldwide, Inc.)

The following table lists the different sections that a report can display and how to use each section:

Report Section	Where It Appears and How to Use It
Report Header and Footer	Appears at the beginning and end of the report. This section is for summary information about the entire report. The report header usually consists of a title, a date, or other information pertinent to the entire report. The report footer may contain summary calculations for the entire report, such as a grand total.
Page Header and Footer	Appears at the top and bottom of each page. The page header and footer may include information such as the name of the report, the date, and the page number, all usually unobtrusively formatted.
Section Header and Footer	Appears at the top and bottom of each grouping and may include data about the particular grouping. Your report may have more than one section and footer — one for each grouping of your data in the report. The section footer may include a subtotal. The formatting of section footers should make the hierarchy of the report obvious (that is, larger fonts for first level groups than for second level groups).
Detail	Appears after each section header, or after the report header if your report has no additional sections. Displays values for each record. The detail section may be repeated many times in a printed report, if the data is grouped. For example, if your report is grouped by date, the detail section displays information for each date group. The detail section may contain calculated fields — for instance, you can create an expression that calculates the total cost for an item (the item cost $\times$ the number of items ordered).

In Report Design view, each section has a specific place. The gray bar names the section, and the items appearing underneath the bar appear each time that section of the report prints.

The report header and footer each print only once, but the page header and footer appear at the top and bottom of each printed page, and the section header and footer and the detail section can appear many times in the report, depending on how the data is grouped.

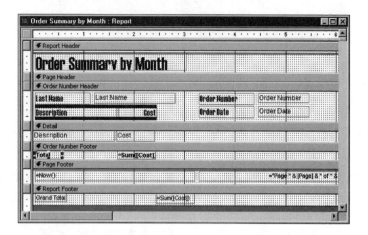

Creating a new section

Before you start creating new sections, you need to have a good understanding of how sections work. Use the Report Wizard to get started with your report and then use the skills discussed in this section to fine-tune your report. *See also* "Creating a Report with the Report Wizard," earlier in this part.

When you create a new report in Design view, you get a three-section report with Page Header, Detail, and Page Footer sections. If you want to add or delete sections, read on. (You can't delete the Detail section, by the way — you'd end up with nothing in your report.)

When you create a new section in a report, you change the way the detail section of the report is grouped. You can't just create a new section before you decide how the new section will group the data in the report — each section is controlled by a field, which is then used to group the Detail section.

To create new sections in your report, display the report in Design view and then click the Sorting and Grouping button on the toolbar (or choose View➪Sorting and Grouping) to display the Sorting and Grouping dialog box. The following steps lead you through the specifics:

1. Click the Sorting and Grouping button on the toolbar. Access displays the Sorting and Grouping dialog box, which displays any fields currently being used for sorting or grouping your report.

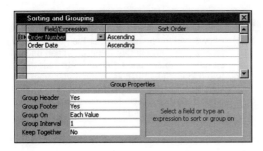

2. To add a section, move your cursor to a blank row and select a field from the Field/Expression drop-down list.

3. Access automatically uses ascending sort order for the new field; if you want to sort in descending order, choose Descending from the Sort Order drop-down list.

4. To make the field a group header, use the Group Properties settings at the bottom of the dialog box. Choose Yes from the Group Header drop-down list. Access adds the grouping symbol to the field in the top part of the dialog box. You may also want to turn the Group Footer on, if you want the section to have a footer.

5. Close the Sorting and Grouping dialog box. Access adds the new section to the report design.

6. Click the Save button to save changes to the report design.

The preceding steps are sufficient to create a new group. The other Group Properties fine-tune the way that the group works. The following table lists the settings in the Group Properties section of the Sorting and Grouping dialog box and what each does.

Group Property	*What It Does*
Group Header	Allows you to choose whether you want the report to contain a Header section for this group. Choose Yes or No from the drop-down list.
Group Footer	Allows you to choose whether you want the report to contain a Footer section for this group. Choose Yes or No from the drop-down list.
Group On	Allows you to choose the size of the group. If the field you're using to group by contains dates, for example, you can group by each value or by day, week, month, year, and so on.
Group Interval	Allows you to choose the size of the interval from the drop-down list. You must have chosen an option other than Each Value from the Group On list.

(continued)

Group Property	What It Does
Keep Together	Allows you to choose whether the group should appear all on one page, or whether the section can be split and printed on more than one page. Select No to split the section over two pages. Select Whole Group if you want the section to always appear on one page. Select With First Detail if you want the group header to always appear on the same page with at least one detail record.

An alternative to grouping records is to hide duplicate data. *See also* "Hiding Duplicate Data," in this part.

Deleting a section

Be aware that when you delete a section, you also delete all the controls in the field.

To remove a section, display the report in Design view and follow these steps:

1. Click the Sorting and Grouping button on the toolbar. Access displays the Sorting and Grouping dialog box, with the names of fields used for sorting and grouping. Fields used for grouping appear with the grouping icon to their left.

2. Select the row for the group that you want to delete. The easiest way is to click that little grouping icon.

3. Press the Delete key. Access asks whether you're sure that you want to delete the group and all the controls in the group.

4. If you're sure, click Yes.

5. Close the Sorting and Grouping dialog box.

Adding and deleting report headers and footers

If you want to add a report header and a report footer to your report, all you need to do is display the report in Design view and then choose View⇔Report Header/Footer. When the report header and footer appear, a check mark appears beside the Report Header/Footer option on the menu.

To get rid of the report header and footer, choose View⇔Report Header/Footer again to turn the check mark off.

If you want to display only a report header, change the height of the footer to zero by clicking and dragging the bottom border of the footer up to the top border of the footer. Perform the same actions with a report header to delete the header from your report.

Adding and deleting page headers and footers

If you want to add or delete the page header and page footer, display the report in Design view and choose View⇨Page Header/Footer.

If you want just a page header or just a footer, change the height of the section that you don't want to use to zero by clicking and dragging the bottom border of the section up to the top border of the section.

You can tell Access not to print the page header and footer on the first and last pages of the report. Why would you want to do so, you ask? Because the page header and footer sometimes repeat information that's already included in the report header and footer (which appear on the first and last pages), so having both on the same page may be redundant.

You can specify which pages the page header and footer print on using the Report Properties dialog box. Display this dialog box by double-clicking the report selector (the gray box in the top-left corner of the Report design, to the left of the horizontal ruler). Then change the Page Header and Page Footer settings to indicate where you want the page header and footer to print, as follows:

✦ **All Pages:** Prints on all pages

✦ **Not with Rpt Hdr:** Does not print on the same page as the report header

✦ **Not with Rpt Ftr:** Does not print on the same page as the report footer

✦ **Not with Rpt Hdr/Ftr:** Does not print on the same page as either the report header or the report footer

Changing the size of a section

You can change the size of a section easily. Move the mouse pointer to the bottom edge of the section; the pointer turns into a funny-looking double-headed arrow. When you see the new pointer shape, click and drag the border up or down to make the section smaller or larger.

Controlling the properties of a section

Each section of a report has properties that you can modify. To display the properties for a section, double-click the section header, the gray bar with the section title. (*See also* "Selecting Parts of the Report," in this part.) Or you can right-click the header bar for the section and choose Properties from the short-cut menu. Once Properties are displayed, you can display the properties for a different section by clicking within that section.

A Properties box pops up, which lets you view and modify the properties for a section. (Report header, report footer, page header, and page footer sections have fewer properties than other sections.)

Use the All tab if you want to see all the settings in any properties dialog box. The other tabs show a subset of settings related to the title of the tab.

The following table describes the most useful section properties:

Property	What It Does
Name	Displays the name that Access gave the section.
Force New Page	Allows you to tell Access to start a new page before this section or after this section.
New Row or Col	Works like the Force New Page setting when you're printing the report in columns.
Keep Together	Allows Access to put page breaks where they occur naturally (No) or forces Access to keep the entire section on one page (Yes).
Visible	Does what it sounds like; set this property to No if you don't want to see the section.
Can Grow	Designates whether the section can get larger to accommodate more data in a control in the section (the control Can Grow property must also be set to Yes). *See also* "Editing Objects in a Report."
Can Shrink	Enables the section to get smaller if the space is not needed; used in conjunction with the Can Shrink setting for a control. *See also* "Editing Objects in a Report."
Tag	Stores additional identifying information about the section.

Editing Objects in a Report

To edit any part of a report, you first must display the report in Design view, which you can accomplish by taking one of the following actions:

✦ Select the report in the Reports tab of the Database window and then click the Design button

✦ Click the View: Design button when you preview the report

To edit any object in a report, you first have to select it. Clicking an object is the best way to select it. *See also* "Selecting Parts of a Report," in this part.

You can change the wording of a label by selecting the label control and then clicking the label again or pressing F2. Access displays a pop-up box with a cursor — use Delete and Backspace to delete

unneeded characters and type any new characters. Press Enter to
put the changes on the report; press Esc to cancel your edits.

 You may also want to use the control's properties to edit it. To
display the properties for a control, double-click the control, or
select it and click the Properties button on the toolbar. You see
different properties depending on the type of control you're
working with. The following table lists the properties that you're
likely to find useful:

Control Property	What It Does
Name	Displays the name of the control.
Caption	Displays the contents of a label control.
Control Source	Displays the name of the field bound to (displayed in) the control.
Format	Displays the format option for the control.
Can Grow	Allows the control to grow vertically when the data doesn't fit in the space allotted. When Can Grow is set to No, only the data that fits in the allotted space appears on the report.
Can Shrink	Allows the control to shrink when less space is needed to display the data.

You can delete any object in a report by selecting it and then
pressing the Del key.

You may also want to change the font, font size, or alignment of a
control. For details, *see also* "Changing Font and Font Size,"
"Creating a Report Using Design View," and "Aligning Report
Objects," in this part. For instructions on moving or changing the
size of a control, *see also* "Changing the Size of an Object" and
"Moving an Object," both in this part.

Formatting Reports with AutoFormat

With AutoFormat, you can apply the same predefined formats that
you saw in the Report Wizard to your report. You have to tell
Access which part of the report you want to format — you can
choose the whole report, one section, or even just one control.

Here's how to use AutoFormat to format your report:

1. Display the report in Design view.

2. Select the part of the report that you want to format with
AutoFormat.

   See also "Selecting Parts of a Report," later in this part.

3. Click the AutoFormat button. Access displays the AutoFormat dialog box.

4. Choose the format you want from the Report AutoFormats list.

5. Click OK to apply the format to the selected part of the report.

Some additional options appear in the AutoFormat dialog box. If you click the Options button, Access displays check boxes that allow you to choose attributes of AutoFormat: Font, Color, and Border. The default is to apply all three, but you can choose not to apply the fonts, colors, or borders in the AutoFormat to your report by clicking to remove the check mark from the formatting option you don't want Access to apply to your report.

The Customize button displays the Customize AutoFormat dialog box, where you can create and delete AutoFormats. You can create your own format based on the current format of the selection or change the AutoFormat so that it matches the format of the current selection.

Grouping Controls

Access 2000 allows you to group controls. Once grouped, you can move all the controls or change the properties of the controls all at once. If you are grouping controls that hold different types of data, however (such as text and numeric), it's usually a good idea to set the control properties before grouping the controls.

To group controls, select them by clicking the first and Shift+clicking additional controls (*see also* "Selecting Parts of a Report," in this part). Then choose Format⇨Group. Once the controls are grouped, select any control in the group to select the whole group.

If you want to change any characteristic of one control in the group, you need to ungroup the controls. To ungroup the controls, select the group and choose Format⇨Ungroup.

Hiding Duplicate Data

Hide Duplicates is a control property that allows you to prevent repetition in your report without defining groups (or additional groups).

For example, I created the following report from a query — it has no groups:

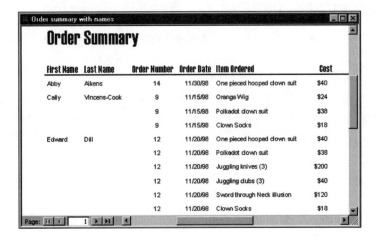

I would rather the first and last name not be repeated for each
item ordered, as in this report:

To prevent the data from repeating, follow these steps:

1. Display the report in Design view.

2. Display the Properties for a text box which has repeating data
   that you don't want on the report. (Display the Properties by
   right-clicking the text box and choosing Properties.)

3. Change the Hide Duplicates Yes.

4. Change the Hide Duplicates property of any other text boxes
   with duplicate data that you want to hide.

Inserting Page Breaks in a Report

You can add a page break to a report in Design view. Follow these steps:

1. Click the Page Break button in the toolbox.

2. Move the pointer to the part of the design where you want the page break and click the mouse button.

Access inserts a page break, which looks like a series of dots that are slightly darker than the grid.

Take care where you insert a page break into a report design — you're working with the design, so the break repeats itself. A good place to use a page break is at the end of a section. For example, if you have records grouped by month and you want each month on a separate page, put the page break at the bottom of the Date Footer section in Design view.

Moving a Control

You can move a control by dragging it. Follow these steps:

1. Select the object you want to move. Anchors appear around the selected object.

See also "Selecting Parts of a Report," in this part.

2. Move the mouse pointer to the edge of the box. The pointer changes into a hand to indicate that you can move the selected objects.

3. Click and drag the objects to where you want them.

To move just one control when the control is paired (like a label and a field control) click and drag the large handle that appears at the top left corner of the object.

Access gives you some other ways to fine-tune the location of a control in a report. You can do the following things:

✦ Use the grid (the dots) to align a control. If you choose Format➪Snap to Grid, Access makes sure that the top left corner of every control lines up with a dot in the grid. If you turn Snap to Grid off (by choosing it again), you can move a control anywhere in the report.

✦ You can align controls by selecting all the objects that you want to align and choosing Format➪Align. The submenu allows you to align objects by the Left, Right, Top, or Bottom edge. You also can use the submenu to align any selected object To Grid.

✦ Use the horizontal and vertical spacing commands to space a group of selected objects evenly. Select the objects that you want to space evenly; then choose Format➪Horizontal Spacing➪Make Equal or Format➪Vertical Spacing➪Make Equal.

See also "Grouping Controls," in this part.

Playing with Borders

You can change the appearance of the border surrounding an object not only by changing its color, but also by changing the width and the style of the border.

To change the width of the border (that is, the thickness of the line), follow these steps:

1. Select the object.

2. Click the arrow next to the Line/Border Width button. Access displays a drop-down list of border-width options. The first option is an invisible border.

3. Click the border thickness that you want to use. Access changes the border of the selected object to match the border that you select.

To change the style of the border, use the Special Effects button. Follow these steps:

1. Select the object.

2. Click the arrow next to the Special Effects button. Access displays some options.

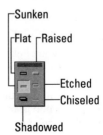

3. Click the option that you want to use.

Because the options in the drop-down list don't give you a very good idea of how the option will appear in your report, the best way to see an effect is to try it.

Previewing Your Report

Reports have two views: Design view and Print Preview. In Design view you tell Access what you want to see in your report, and how you want it organized. Print Preview allows you to see how the report will look on paper.

To display the print preview of a report, click the View button or the Print Preview button on the toolbar.

See also "Creating a Report Using Design View," in this part.

See also "Previewing Before You Print," in Part VII. Flip to that topic to find out how to navigate your report in Print Preview and how to zoom in and out to see more and less of the report at one time.

Selecting Parts of a Report

You have to be in Design view to select part of a report. You can select an entire section (such as the Report Header or the Details section) or a single object.

Selecting controls

Select a *control* (an object in a report) by clicking it. Selected objects have anchors (small black boxes) around them.

These are other methods for selecting controls that you may find useful:

✦ Select more than one control at a time by clicking and dragging a rectangle that includes the controls you want to select.

Select more than one control by clicking the first control that you want to select; then Shift+clicking additional controls.

✦ Click the vertical or horizontal ruler. When you click the horizontal ruler at the top of the Design view window, you select all the objects that appear at that point in the design. For instance, if you click the one-inch mark on the ruler, all the objects that appear on the vertical line one inch in from the margin are selected. You can use the vertical ruler on the left of the Design view to select all the objects in one row of the design.

✦ Select a control from the Object box in the Formatting toolbar. Click the arrow next to the box to see a list of all objects in the report. Click the control that you want to select. Access displays anchors around that control.

Deselect controls by clicking somewhere in the grid of the design where no control appears. If you want to deselect one of several selected controls, Shift+click the control to deselect it and leave the other controls selected.

Selecting a section of the report

To select a section of the report, like the Report Header or the Detail section, click the section selector. To select the entire report, click the report selector.

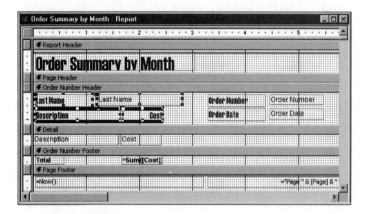

Sending a Report to Another Application

 Microsoft makes it very easy for you to send a report (or a datasheet, for that matter) to another Microsoft application. All you need to do is click the OfficeLinks button, which appears on the Print Preview toolbar. The OfficeLinks default application is Word, but you can select Excel from the drop-down list.

When you click the OfficeLinks button, Access saves your report in the format that you've chosen (word processing document or spreadsheet), opens the chosen application, and displays your report. Then you can edit, analyze, or print your report in that application.

 You may prefer to use the drag and drop functionality to exchange data with Excel. You can drag Access tables and queries from the database window to Excel. You can also select portions of a datasheet and drag them to Excel.

Sorting Records in a Report

You *can* sort a report by sorting the table or query that generated the fields in the report. But a more foolproof method is to use the Sorting and Grouping dialog box.

One method to sort records is to group them. When you tell Access to group by using a certain field, you get sorting thrown in for free. If you want to use a field to sort records without using it to group records, you still get to use the Sorting and Grouping dialog box.

Here's how to use the Sorting and Grouping dialog box to sort the records in a report:

 1. Display the Sorting and Grouping dialog box by clicking the Sorting and Grouping button on the toolbar. Access displays the Sorting and Grouping dialog box, with fields used for grouping marked by the Grouping icon.

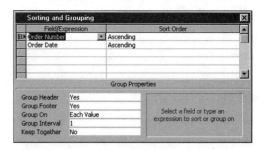

2. Click a blank row, and add a field that you want to use for sorting by selecting it from the drop-down list.

3. If you don't want to sort in ascending order, press Tab to move to the Sort Order setting and choose Descending from the drop-down list.

4. Close the dialog box.

By not giving the field a group header or footer, you use it only for sorting, not for grouping.

Part VI

Forms and Data Access Pages for Displaying and Entering Data

Unlike tables, forms display only the fields you want to see. You can create a format for a form that shows all the data for one record on the screen at one time — something that is difficult to do when you have a number of fields in a table. You can also add features such as check boxes and drop-down lists that make entering data easier.

Also covered in this part are Data Access Pages, which allow you to edit and enter data through a Web page you create with Access. Data Access Pages are a new feature in Access 2000. They provide a way to work with the data in a database without opening the database in Access — instead you use Internet Explorer 5.

In this part . . .

- ✔ Creating AutoForms
- ✔ Creating an AutoPage
- ✔ Creating forms with the Form Wizard
- ✔ Creating a Data Access Page with a wizard
- ✔ Entering data in a form
- ✔ Formatting a form with AutoFormat
- ✔ Adding objects to your form
- ✔ Changing tab order
- ✔ Refining your form in Design view

About Data Access Pages

Data Access Pages are similar to forms — they present data and allow the user to edit existing data and enter new records. However, rather than working with data from within the database, Data Access Pages allow you to use Internet Explorer 5 to work with data on an intranet or on the Internet. Users of Data Access Pages need both Microsoft Internet Explorer 5 and a Microsoft Access 2000 license.

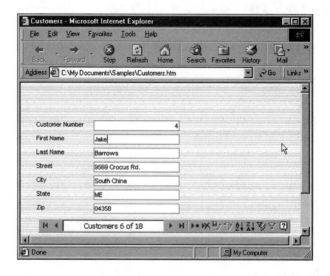

Here are a few things you should keep in mind about Data Access Pages:

+ Data Access Pages can be used for different purposes. For instance, you may use a Data Access Page to allow the user to view data, enter data, or analyze data. Depending on the purpose, the features of the Data Access Page will differ. The data may be interactive, or it may not allow changes. You may incorporate *expand indicators*, which allow summary data to be viewed and then expanded to view detail material. You may allow users to sort and filter data. You may include a PivotTable or chart to enable easier analysis. You may want to create a Web page that has some information on it and then add Data Access Page controls to it.

+ Unlike other Access objects, Data Access Pages are not stored within Access — they are HTML files stored in the same folder as the database file. However, Access automatically creates shortcuts to the Data Access Pages associated with the database and displays those shortcuts in the Pages view of the Database window.

✦ Data Access Pages are similar to forms and reports. They are made up of controls that you put on the report in Design view. Like designing reports and forms, you use the field list, toolbox, controls, and the Sorting and Grouping dialog box to design a Data Access Page. However, although the Data Access Page Design view is similar to the Design view for reports and forms, there are many differences, mainly because you are not ultimately creating an Access object but an HTML object.

You can create a Data Access Page in four ways:

✦ Create from scratch

✦ Use a wizard

✦ Create an AutoPage

✦ Open an existing HTML file with in Data Access Page Design view so that you can add controls to display data from your database

About Forms

Forms are similar to reports, except that *forms* enable you to input and edit data, not just view and print it. You can easily create a form that enables you to work with linked tables — you can see and enter related data in the same place, and you can see all the fields in one record at the same time, instead of having to scroll across a table. You can also create different forms for different people or groups of people who use a database.

Forms can range from relatively simple to complex. Really extravagant forms can include formatting, calculated fields, and controls (such as check boxes, buttons, and pictures) that make entering data easier.

See also Part V. Forms are so similar to reports that many of the features you use to create a form are the same features you use to create a report.

Adding a Form to Your Database

The best way to create a form is to start with the Form Wizard — especially if you want to create a form that includes data from more than one table or query. Once the Wizard finishes, you can edit the form in Design view. **See also** "Adding a Form with the Form Wizard," in this part.

Making a new form is similar to making any new Access object. The easiest way to create a new form is to follow these steps:

 1. Display the Forms view in the Database window.

2. Click the <u>N</u>ew button. Access displays the New Form dialog box, which gives you several choices for creating your form.

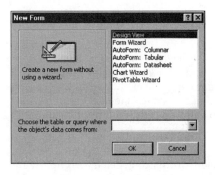

3. Choose the method you want to use to create the form.

4. Select the table or query on which you want to base the form.

5. Click OK.

The following table describes the choices on the New Form dialog box and tells you when to use each of them.

Option in New Form Dialog Box	When to Use It
Design View	When you want to design your own form from scratch, with no help from Access. (Design view is great for putting your own stamp on a form, but getting started with a wizard really helps.)
Form Wizard	When you want help creating a form. The Form Wizard walks you through the creation of a form, enabling you to use fields from multiple tables and queries, to create groups, and to perform calculations for summary fields. The resulting form is bland, but editing an existing form is much easier than creating one from scratch.
AutoForm: Columnar	When you want to create a quick and easy columnar form (the field names go in one column and the data in another) from the table or query you specify.
AutoForm: Tabular	When you want to create a quick and easy tabular form from the table or query that you specify. A tabular form displays data in rows, like a datasheet, but with more room for each row.
AutoForm: Datasheet	When you want to create a datasheet form from the table or query that you specify. These forms look almost exactly like a datasheet. (Tabular AutoForms are similar, but a little spiffier.)
Chart Wizard	When you want to create a form consisting of a chart.
PivotTable Wizard	When you want to create a form with an Excel PivotTable.

 You don't have to use the New button in the Forms tab of the Database window to create a new form; you can also use the New Object button. In fact, the default setting for the New Object button is an AutoForm. You can also display the button's drop-down list and choose Form. The AutoForm option creates a Columnar AutoForm from the data in the table or query selected in the Database window.

 The quick way to create a form from a table or query is to select the name of the table or query that you want to use in the Database window and then click the New Object button and select Form or AutoForm.

Choosing Insert⇨Form or Insert⇨AutoForm also creates a new form.

Adding a Form with the Form Wizard

The Form Wizard is a great way to create a simple or complex form — but especially a complex form. If you want to use fields from multiple tables in your form, the Form Wizard is the way to go.

See also "Working with Wizards," in Part I.

Here's how to create a form using the Form Wizard:

1. Display the Forms view of the Database window and double-click the Create Form by Using Wizard button. Access displays the first window of the Form Wizard, where you can choose the fields that you want to use in the form.

2. Use the Tables/Queries drop-down list to choose the first table or query from which you want to use fields.

3. Select the fields in the Available Fields list that you want to appear on the form and move them to the Selected Fields list by double-clicking, or by selecting a field and clicking the right-arrow button.

4. Repeat Steps 3 and 4 to select fields from other tables or queries.

5. When all the fields that you want to display in the form appear in the Selected Fields box, click Next. The Form Wizard displays the next window. If you selected fields from only one table, this window asks you to choose a format for the form — skip right to Step 9. Otherwise, the window asks how you want to group your data.

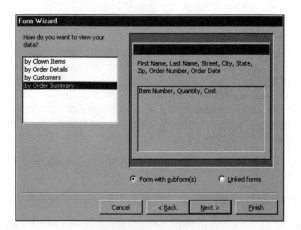

6. Choose the organization that you want for your form by double-clicking the table or query by which you want to group records. Grouping items in a form is similar to grouping fields in a report. In the preceding figure, for example, many items are related to a single order, so grouping the data according to

the data in the Order Summary table displays the summary information for the order only once, and then shows all the items ordered (grouped by the catalog from which they were ordered) and the specific information about the order.

7. Choose Form with Subforms(s) or Linked Forms from the radio buttons at the bottom of the window. If you want to see all the fields on the form at one time, click the Form with Subform(s) radio button. If you click Linked Forms, Access creates a separate form for the detail records. Users can then view this form by clicking a button in the first form. (If you're not sure which option to choose, go for Form with Subforms(s).)

8. Click Next to see the next window. Access displays a window that enables you to choose the layout for the form or subform, if you're creating one.

9. Choose the layout. You can click a layout option to see what it looks like. If you're not sure which layout to use, stick with Columnar — it's easy to use and easy to edit. If you're working with grouped fields, this window gives you only two options: Tabular and Datasheet.

10. Click Next to see the next window, which enables you to choose a style for the form.

11. Choose one of the lovely styles that the Form Wizard offers. Click a style to see a sample of a form formatted with that style. None of the styles is gorgeous, so pick one and get on with the real work.

12. Click Next to see the final window.

13. Give the form a name, and decide whether you want to see the form itself (Open the form to view or enter information) or the form Design view (Modify the form's design). If you're creating subforms or linked forms, Access enables you to name those items, too (or you can accept the names that Access gives them).

14. Click Finish to create the form.

```
Order Summary                                        _ □ ×
First Name    Madeline          Zip              04357
Last Name     Molkenbur         Order Number           3
Street        15 Hydrangea St.  Order Date       10/6/98
City          Poland
State         ME
Order Details    Item Ordered        Quantity       Cost
            ▶ Juggling clubs (3)  ▼         1    $40.00
              Buttons clown suit  ▼         1   $190.00
            *                     ▼
            Record: I◀ ◀      1  ▶ ▶I ▶* of 2
Record: I◀ ◀      5  ▶ ▶I ▶* of 15
```

Adding a Page with the Page Wizard

The Page Wizard is a great way to create simple or complex Data
Access Pages. If you want to use fields from multiple tables in your
form, the Page Wizard is the way to go.

See also "Working with Wizards," in Part I.

Here's how to create a page using the Page Wizard:

1. Display the Pages view of the Database window and double-
   click the Create Data Access Page by Using Wizard icon.
   Access displays the first window of the Page Wizard, where
   you can choose the fields that you want to use in the form.

2. Use the Tables/Queries drop-down list to choose the first
   table or query from which you want to use fields.

3. Select the fields in the Available Fields list that you want to
   appear on the form and move them to the Selected Fields list
   by double-clicking, or by selecting a field and clicking the
   right-arrow button.

4. Repeat Steps 2 and 3 to select fields from other tables or
   queries.

5. When all the fields that you want to display in the form appear
   in the Selected Fields box, click Next. The Page Wizard
   displays the next window, which asks how you want to group
   your data.

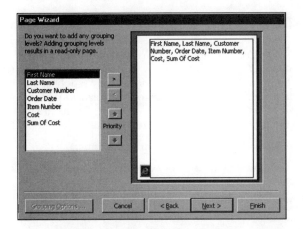

If you add grouping levels, you create a read-only page. That means that the Data Access Page cannot be used to edit and enter data. Only a page with no groups can be used to edit and enter data.

6. Choose the organization that you want for your page by double-clicking the field by which you want to group data.

7. Click Next to see the next window. Access displays a window that enables you to choose the sort order for the page.

8. To specify a sort order, display the drop-down list of field names next to the box labeled "1" and choose a field to sort by. Click the Sort button to change the sort order from ascending (A to Z, 1 to 10) to descending (Z to A, 10 to 1). Click the button again to change the sort order back. You can sort by up to four fields — use the additional boxes to specify additional fields on which to sort. Additional sort fields are used only when the initial sort field is identical for two or more records — then the next sort field is used to determine in what order to display those records.

9. Click Next to see the final window.

10. Give the page a name, and decide whether you want to see the page itself (Open the Page) or the page Design view (Modify the Page's Design). If you want to add a theme, select the Do You Want To Apply A Theme To Your Page check box.

11. Click Finish to create the page.

The form you create exists only in Access. When you close the page, Access asks you if you want to save the page — this time as an .htm file separate from the database.

Adding an AutoForm

AutoForms are a quick, easy way to create a form based on one table or query. AutoForms even know how to handle repeated information which may appear in a query (such as multiple items in one order), and they section off the form so that you see the repeated information only once. But AutoForms are easiest to use and understand when you create them using just one table.

Access provides three flavors of AutoForms:

✦ **Columnar:** This type of AutoForm has one record per page.

✦ **Tabular:** Tabular AutoForms are convenient, but I can't go any farther than that. These forms look like generic tables, with field names at the top and the data for each record in a nice, wide row. When you use a Tabular AutoForm, expect to do a little resizing of the controls in Design view. Access uses a standard size for the controls — they may not fit your labels and data.

If you use a query that links related data from multiple tables to create a Tabular AutoForm, Access does its best, but the result doesn't look much like a straightforward Tabular AutoForm. If your data comes from more than one table, try the Form Wizard, instead. The Form Wizard enables you to choose how to group repeated data.

✦ **Datasheet:** A Datasheet AutoForm looks exactly like a table. This type of AutoForm can be useful for subforms that you want to display in compact list form.

To create an AutoForm, follow these steps:

1. In the Database window, select the table or query on which you want to base the form.

2. To create a Columnar AutoForm, click the New Object: AutoForm button. Access immediately creates the Columnar AutoForm. To create another kind of AutoForm, choose Form from the New Object drop-down list. Access displays the New Form dialog box.

3. Choose the type of AutoForm you want to create, and click OK. Access creates the form.

If you don't like the background that Access chooses for your AutoForm, you can easily change it by using AutoFormat. *See also* "Formatting Your Form with AutoFormat," in this part.

Adding an AutoPage to Your Report

The easiest type of Data Access Page to create is an AutoPage. Similar to an AutoReport and an AutoForm, AutoPage simply takes the fields on the table or query you provide it with and creates a Data Access Page.

To create a columnar AutoPage, follow these steps:

1. Display the Pages view in the Database window.

2. Click the New button to display the New Data Access Page dialog box.

3. Select AutoPage: Columnar.

4. Select the table or query that contains the data you want shown on the page.

5. Click OK. Access creates the page and displays it in Design view.

6. Save the page by clicking the Save button on the toolbar. Because each Data Access Page is stored in an HTML file separate from the database, you must provide a name for the new file on the Save As Data Access Page dialog box. You may also choose to save the file in a folder other than the folder where the database is saved.

Click the View button to see the page in Page view.

Adding Subforms to Your Form

Use subforms to display related data from different tables. The main form in the following figure displays the "one" side of a one-to-many relationship. The subform (the bottom half of the form) displays the records in the "many" side of the relationship.

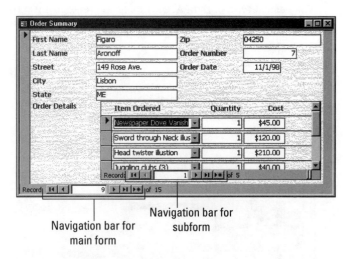

Navigation bar for
main form

Navigation bar for
subform

Notice that the form has two navigation bars: one for the main form and one for the subform.

The easiest way to create a form with subforms is to have the Form Wizard do the hard work for you. You can always edit and improve the form later.

If you want to create a main form with a subform, follow these steps:

1. Create the main form and display it in Design view.

 2. Click the Subform/Subreport button in the Toolbox to tell Access that you want to add the subform to the main form.

3. In the form design, click and drag the mouse to create a box in which the subform will appear. Access launches the Subform/Subreport Wizard to lead you through the process of creating a subform.

AutoFormatting Your Form

 You can use AutoFormat to give your form one of the format styles that Access provides. The styles you see in the AutoFormat dialog box are the same ones you see in the Form Wizard.

To format your form, you first have to select what you want to format: the entire form, part of the form, or even just one control. Selecting part of a form in Design view is identical to selecting part of a report in Design view. *See also* "Selecting Parts of a Report," in Part V to brush up on how to select a control or a section of a form or report.

To use AutoFormat to format your form, follow these steps:

1. Display the form in Design view.

2. Select the part of the form that you want to format with AutoFormat.

 3. Click the AutoFormat button in the toolbar. Access displays the AutoFormat dialog box.

4. Select the format that you want to use. You can select a format to see an example of how your form looks formatted.

5. Click OK to apply the format to the part of the form that you selected in Step 2.

See also "Formatting Reports with AutoFormat," in Part V.

Editing and Formatting Forms

The steps for creating, editing, and formatting form controls are identical to performing the same tasks with report controls. The following topics in Part V also apply to forms.

However, some formatting tasks are even easier with forms than with reports because they can be done from the Form view without switching to the Design view.

You can do the following formatting in Form view:

✦ Change control properties: Right-click the control and choose Properties to display the properties.

✦ Change font.

✦ Change font size.

✦ Change text appearance using the bold, italic, and underline buttons.

The formatting toolbar is normally displayed in Form view (unless you turn it off), and any of the buttons can be used to format the selected control. Note that in Form view there is no visual clue that a control is selected — the selected control is the last one you click. Design view is superior for making wholesale changes because only one control at a time can be selected in Form view, but the new feature makes on-the-fly editing possible in Form view.

Entering Data through a Form

After you create a form, you want to use it for its intended purpose: viewing and entering data. To use a form that you created, double-click the form name in the Database window — you're now in Form view. The data that a form displays comes directly from tables in the database, and any changes that you make in that data are reflected in the table. When you add data by using a form, the data is added to the table.

In general, you use the same skills to work with a form as you use to work with datasheets. You can use navigation buttons at the bottom of the form or subform to move to different records, and you press the Tab or Enter key to move from one field to another. *See also* "Moving Around in a Datasheet," in Part III.

If you prefer to use the keyboard to move around a form, the following table lists the keys to use and where they move the cursor.

To Move Here in a Form . . .	Press This Key
Following field	Tab, Enter, or →
Preceding field	Shift + Tab or ←
First field of current record	Home
Last field of current record	End
Subform	Ctrl + Tab

To Move Here in a Form . . .	Press This Key
Main form	Ctrl+Shift+Tab
New record	Ctrl+plus sign (+)

Inserting Controls

To put controls on your form design, follow the same procedure you would follow to put controls on a report. *See also* "Adding a Control," in Part V.

Inserting Formulas in Forms

The procedure for putting a calculation in a form is identical to the way you put a calculation in a report. *See also* "Adding Calculations to a Report," in Part V.

Modifying Tab Order

When entering data in a form, you press Tab to move to the next field. *Tab order* specifies which field the cursor moves to next.

When you create a form, Access designates a tab order. You can change the tab order that Access creates by following these steps:

1. Display the form in Design view.

2. Choose View⇨Tab Order. Access displays the Tab Order dialog box.

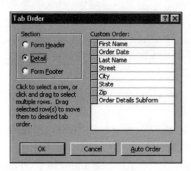

3. Drag the fields so that they appear in the order most useful for entering data.

4. Close the dialog box.

Selecting Part of a Form

You select part of a form the same way that you select part of a report. First, you must view the form in Design view. ***See also*** "Selecting Parts of a Report," in Part V.

Viewing Your Form in Design View

If you want to work on the design of your form, you have to display the form in Design view.

 You can now change control properties without displaying the form in Design view — change properties from the Form view by right-clicking the control and choosing Properties from the shortcut menu.

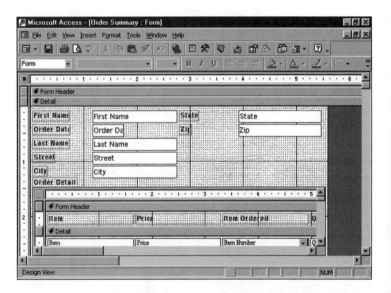

You can display the Design view of a form by doing either of the following things:

✦ Selecting the form in the Forms tab of the Database window and clicking the Design button.

 ✦ Clicking the Design View button when you're working with the form in Form view.

The formatting toolbar and the toolbox also appear in report Design view. ***See also*** "Creating a Report Using Design View," in Part V.

Part VII

Printing Your Work for the World to See

Although Access does a marvelous job of giving you results on-screen, you sometimes need to get those results on paper. After all, it's not always convenient to drag your boss out of her office, down the hall, and into your cubicle so that she can see the analysis that she's been bothering you about for so long. You can't get around it — you have to know how to print. And because Access provides so many ways to make an analysis fancy, isn't it appropriate to make the printout look fancy, too?

Printing from Access is fundamentally the same whether you're printing a table, query, form, or report. This part covers all the ins and outs of printing — from previewing your print job to choosing a printer to actually printing your masterpiece — as well as dozens of little extras.

In this part . . .

- ✔ Stopping the printer in its tracks
- ✔ Setting paper size and orientation
- ✔ Previewing your print job
- ✔ Printing an object
- ✔ Printing only the part you want

Canceling a Print Job

If you have a printer directly connected to your computer, you get two chances to cancel a print job. The first chance is when you see a small dialog box telling you that your table (or report or whatever) is printing. The dialog box includes a Cancel button that you can click to cancel the print job.

The printer doesn't stop printing immediately, and may print out another page or two, but clicking the Cancel button stops Access from sending more information to the printer.

If you want to stop a print job after the dialog box with the Cancel button disappears, you have to resort to the fallback method — using the Windows Printer window. When any document is printing in Windows, a small printer appears in the indicators box in the taskbar. (The *indicators box* usually appears on the right of the taskbar and contains the time.) Double-click that small printer icon to display the Windows Printer window — a window that contains the name of your printer on the title bar and lists current print jobs.

If the printer you use is on a network, you may not be able to use the Printer window to cancel a print job. You should identify your network guru (or someone who knows how to cancel print jobs) to find out how to cancel a print job on your network.

To cancel a print job from the Printer window, follow these steps:

1. Right-click the name of the document that you want to cancel to display the shortcut menu.

2. Choose Cancel Printing from the shortcut menu. The printer stops printing.

Changing Margins

You can change the margins of your printout by using the Page Setup dialog box.

You can display the Page Setup dialog box in two ways:

✦ Click the Setup button in the Print dialog box.

✦ Choose File⇨Page Setup.

To change margins, display the object you want to print and follow these steps:

1. Display the Page Setup dialog box by choosing File⇨Page Setup and click the Margins tab.

2. Click the setting for the margin that you want to change.

3. Edit the value. (You don't have to type the inch marks; Access adds them for you.)

4. If you want to change another margin, press Tab to move the cursor to another margin setting. When you move to another option, the sample area of the Page Setup dialog box updates to show you how your new margin will look on paper.

5. Click OK when you finish with the Page Setup dialog box.

Choosing Paper Size and Orientation

The Page tab of the Page Setup dialog box has settings that tell Access what size paper you're using and whether you want to print in portrait or landscape mode.

Something weird is going on in Access. You can display the Page Setup dialog box in two ways, but to see the Page tab, you have to choose File⇨Page Setup. Clicking the Setup button in the Print dialog box does not display the Page tab.

Changing paper size

If you're printing on paper other than the standard 8^1/$_2$ x 11-inch size, you have to tell Access about it.

To tell Access about the size of the paper you're printing on, view the object you want to print and follow these steps:

1. Choose File⇨Page Setup to display the Page Setup dialog box.

2. Click the Page tab at the top of the dialog box.

3. Click the arrow to the right of Size, and select the size of paper that you're using.

4. Click OK to close the dialog box.

Choosing landscape or portrait

You can ask Access to print your data on the paper in either of two ways:

✦ **Portrait orientation:** This setting puts the short side of the paper at the top and bottom (like a notepad or this book). Why does Access call this *portrait* orientation? Most portraits are framed so that the sides are longer than the top and bottom.

✦ **Landscape orientation:** This setting puts the long side of the paper at the top and bottom, so that more data fits across the page. Most computer monitors have the equivalent of landscape orientation, and so do most landscape paintings in your local museum — the artist can fit in more land and less sky that way.

To change the orientation of the paper, view the object you want to print and follow these steps:

1. Choose File⇨Page Setup to display the Page Setup dialog box.

2. Click the Page tab at the top of the dialog box.

3. Click Portrait or Landscape, depending on how you want Access to print.

4. Click OK to close the dialog box.

Displaying the Print Dialog Box

The Print dialog box provides settings that control how much of the chosen object to print, the order in which to print the pages of multiple copies, and which printer to print.

Display the Print dialog box by choosing File⇨Print.

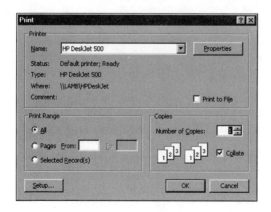

Picking a Printer

If you have multiple printers set up and attached to your computer (perhaps through a network), you can choose the Name option in the Print dialog box to tell Access which printer to print to. Press Ctrl+P to display the Print dialog box and then click the arrow to the right of the Name option and choose the printer that you want to use.

Previewing Before You Print

Always preview before you print. Previewing your work enables you to make sure that the printout is going to look the way you expect it to — you can save a lot of trees this way!

 To preview your print job, click the Print Preview button.

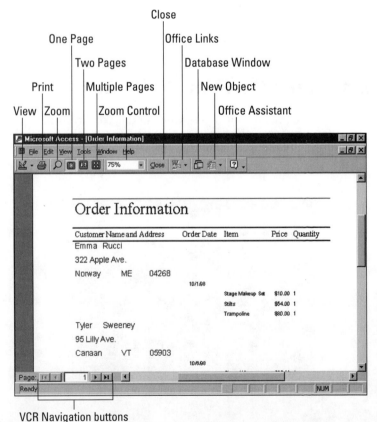

VCR Navigation buttons

Clicking the Print Preview button when you're working with a report is the same as displaying the report (rather than the report design) — reports are either in Design or Print Preview view.

You can click the View button while you're viewing a print preview to see the object in another view — Datasheet view for tables and queries, and Design view for reports and forms.

Navigating a preview

You can get around a print preview in a few ways:

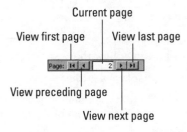

+ Use the scroll bars, when they appear. (Scroll bars appear only when an entire page doesn't fit on the screen.)

+ Use the ←, →, ↑, and ↓ or the PgUp and PgDn keys on the keyboard.

+ Use the VCR navigation buttons at the bottom of the window to view a different page.

+ Use the Current Page option in the VCR navigation buttons to go to a particular page — just select the box, type the number of the page that you want to view, and press Enter to view the page.

Zooming in

You can control how big the pages look in print preview. You may want to zoom in so that you can see whether the font looks good and the figures are exactly right, or you may want to zoom out and see a few pages at the same time to see whether you like the general layout.

Four buttons in the toolbar change the amount of the printout that appears on-screen. The following table shows you the buttons and tells you what each button does to the preview.

Button	What It's Called	What It Does
Zoom	Zoom	Toggles between 100% and One Page view
One Page	One Page	Displays one entire page in the preview window
Two Pages	Two Pages	Displays two pages in the preview window
Multiple Pages	Multiple Pages	Enables you to select from a grid how many pages to display; drag the mouse pointer past the edge of the grid to display a larger grid
Fit	Zoom Control	Enables you to choose your own zoom factor

To use the Multiple Pages button, follow these steps:

1. Click the button. Access displays a grid of pages.

2. Move the mouse pointer so that the number of pages that you want to display are selected. The bottom of the grid tells you how pages are displayed — for example, 2 x 3 displays two rows each of three pages.

The Zoom button enables you to choose among many zoom levels. The larger the zoom percentage, the larger the print appears on-screen — 100 percent is approximately the size that the print will appear on paper. If you choose Fit from the Zoom drop-down list, Access fits one page in the window. You can change the zoom value by doing either of the following things:

✦ Selecting a value from the drop-down list.

✦ Typing a new zoom value in the box and pressing Enter (you don't have to type %). You can choose zoom values of more than 100 percent by typing them.

Printing an Object

Views that you can print have a Print button in the toolbar. Some views (notably Design views) cannot be printed. In those views, the Print button is grayed out, indicating that you can't click it.

 Although you can't print the Design view of a table, query, report, or form, you can print definitions for these objects. Choose Tools⇨ Analyze⇨Documenter to open the Documenter dialog box. You can print an object such as a datasheet or a report in three ways:

✦ To print the object currently on your screen without changing any settings, click the Print button.

✦ If you want to change some settings in the Print dialog box before printing the object, choose File⇨Print or press Ctrl+P. Change settings as necessary and click OK to print the object.

✦ To print an object without opening it, select it in the Database window and then click the Print button, or right-click the object and then choose Print from the shortcut menu. Access sends the object straight to the printer. To display the Print dialog box first, select the object and choose File⇨Print. Change settings as necessary and click OK to print the object.

Printing specific pages

If you know exactly which pages you want to print, you can use the Print Range option in the Print dialog box to tell Access which pages to print.

To print specific pages, follow these steps:

1. Display the Print dialog box by choosing File⇨Print.

2. In the Print Range section, choose Pages.

3. In the From box, type the number of the first page in the range that you want to print.

4. In the To box, type the number of the last page in the range that you want to print.

5. Click the OK button to print the pages that you specified.

Printing specific records

Depending on the object that you're printing, you can print specified records. Here's how to print just the records you want:

1. Select the records that you want to print.

2. Display the Print dialog box by choosing File⇨Print.

3. In the Print Range section, choose Selected Records. If you didn't select any records in Step 1, Access prints the record that the cursor was in when you displayed the Print dialog box.

4. Click OK to print the records.

Printing and Collating Multiple Copies

If you want to print more than one copy, you can use the Print dialog box to tell Access how many copies to print. Just change the setting of the Number of Copies option.

To change the order in which Access prints the pages, use the Collate option in the Print dialog box.

✦ When you select the Collate option, Access prints a single copy of all the pages before moving on to the next copy.

✦ When you deselect the Collate option, Access prints multiple copies of the first page before moving on to the second page, and so on.

Part VIII

Access 2000 Tips and Tricks

When you pick a way to break up a subject, some useful items always fall through the cracks. Computer book authors either stick those topics in places where they really don't fit, or they create a separate chapter (or, in this case, a part) on those useful tips and tricks.

In this part . . .

- ✔ Backing up your database
- ✔ Checking the spelling of data
- ✔ Copying database objects
- ✔ Cutting, copying, and pasting information
- ✔ Exporting information from your database to another application

Backing Up Your Database

Having a back-up plan for your computer is a necessity, not an option. If you work at home or if you're in charge of backing up your own work at the office, you may want to look at *Windows 98 For Dummies* or *Windows NT 4 For Dummies,* both by Andy Rathbone (IDG Books Worldwide, Inc.).

In the meantime, at least make back-up copies of your Access databases. Each database is stored in a file on a disk, probably your hard disk. Access files have the extension .mdb, the file type Microsoft Access Database, and are usually stored in the C:\My Documents folder, unless you specify that they be stored somewhere else.

The easiest way to create a backup of a database is to use Explorer or My Computer to simply copy the .mdb file (and the .ldb file, if one exists) to a floppy disk or to another hard disk (perhaps a network drive, if one is available). If you can't fit the entire file on one floppy disk, try using a utility like WinZip. WinZip compresses your file and can save it to more than one disk if necessary.

Checking Your Spelling

You can check the spelling of data in a datasheet, form, or query. Here's how:

1. Click the Database Window button on the toolbar to display the Database window.

2. Select a table, form, or query.

3. Click the Spelling button in the toolbar. Access opens the object and displays the Spelling dialog box with the first word that it thinks is misspelled.

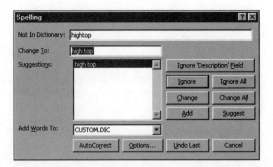

4. To correct the word displayed in the Not In Dictionary box, choose a correctly spelled word from the Suggestions list or type a correctly spelled word in the Change To box and then click Change. Access corrects the misspelled word and looks for the next misspelled word.

You can use buttons in the Spelling dialog box to do much more than just correct spelling. The following table describes what each button does.

Button	What It Does
Ignore *"Fieldname"* Field	Tells Access not to check the spelling of the specified field
Ignore	Skips the current word and finds the next misspelled word
Ignore All	Ignores the word listed in the Not In Dictionary box each time it is found during the current spelling check
Change	Changes the word in the Not In Dictionary box to the word listed in the Change To box
Change All	Changes the word in the Not In Dictionary box to the word listed in the Change To box every time it is found during the current spelling check
Add	Adds the word to the dictionary
Suggest	Suggests more words
AutoCorrect	Adds the misspelled word and the correct spelling to the AutoCorrect list
Options	Displays the Spell Options dialog box where you can tell Access whether to suggest words, whether to ignore certain words, and which dictionary to use (you can specify a foreign language using the Dictionary option)
Undo Last	Undoes the last change made in the Spelling dialog box
Cancel	Closes the Spelling dialog box

Converting a Database

Access 2000 uses a different file format than earlier versions of Access, so you may need to change the database format if someone without Access 2000 needs to use the database. You can convert a database *from* an earlier version of Access or *to* an earlier version of Access.

Converting from an earlier format to Access 2000

If you need to convert a database created with an earlier version of Access, follow these steps:

1. Open Access.

2. Choose Tools⇨Database Utilities⇨Convert Database⇨ To Current Access Database Version from the menu.

Access displays the Database to Convert From dialog box.

3. Select the database you want to convert and click the Convert button.

Access displays the Convert Database Into dialog box.

4. Give the converted database a new File name. You cannot use the name and path of an existing database.

5. Click the Save button to create the converted database.

Converting from Access 2000 to an earlier format

To convert an Access 2000 database to a format useable by an earlier version of Access, follow these steps:

1. Open the database in Access.

2. Choose Tools⇨Database Utilities⇨Convert Database⇨ To Prior Access Database Version.

Access displays the Convert Database Into dialog box.

3. Give the converted database a File Name. You cannot use the name and path of an existing database.

4. Click the Save button to create the converted database.

Copying a Database Object

Copying a database object can provide you with a backup copy in case you make a change that you can't undo. Or you may want to make a copy of a complex object when you are creating another, similar object — then you have an object that you can edit, and you don't have to start from scratch. To copy any database object, follow these steps:

1. Select the object in the database window.

2. Press Ctrl+C or choose Edit⇨Copy from the menu.

3. Press Ctrl+V or choose Edit➪Paste from the menu.

Access displays the Paste dialog box where you name the copied table.

4. Give the object a name. If it is a backup copy, you may want to use the word *backup* in the name.

5. Click OK to create the copy.

When you make a copy of a table by pressing Ctrl+V or choosing Edit➪Paste, you can choose from three Paste Options, as follows:

✦ Structure Only: Copies the table design, but not the data.

✦ Structure and Data: Copies the table design and data.

✦ Append Data to Existing Table: Adds the data to the end of the table named in the Table Name option on the dialog box. The two tables must have the same structure — the same number of fields with the same data types.

Cutting, Copying, and Pasting

Cutting and pasting (or copying and pasting) is a great way to move or copy information from one place in Access to another.

You can use the Cut, Copy, and Paste commands in three ways: by clicking buttons in the toolbar, by choosing commands from the Edit menu, or by pressing shortcut keys. The following table lists menu options, buttons, and keystrokes for cutting, copying, and pasting.

Edit Menu Option	Button	Keystroke
✂	Cut	Ctrl+X
📋	Copy	Ctrl+C
📋	Paste	Ctrl+V

To copy or cut and paste something, follow these steps:

1. Select the data or object that you want to cut or copy.

2. Choose your favorite method to cut or copy what you selected (Ctrl+X and Ctrl+C are mine). When you cut something, it disappears from the screen and is stored in the Windows Clipboard. When you copy something, it stays where it is, and Access also places a copy in the Windows Clipboard.

3. Move the cursor to the place where you want the item to appear.

4. Choose your favorite method to paste the item. (Ctrl+V works well.)

You can use the Office Clipboard to copy and paste more than one item at a time. (Previously, only one item could be stored in the clipboard, and any cut or copied item replaced the contents of the clipboard.)

If you cut or copy more than one item without pasting any, Access displays the Clipboard toolbar, which can store up to 12 items. The clipboard can store items from all Office applications — Access, Excel, Word, Outlook, and PowerPoint.

The Clipboard toolbar displays one icon for each stored item. To see the first 50 characters of the stored items rest the pointer over the icon on the toolbar. You can paste any item in the clipboard to the cursor's position by clicking the appropriate icon on the toolbar. The Paste All button pastes all the stored items.

Importing and Exporting Data

You may want to get data stored in another application and use it in your Access database. Conversely, you may want to use data from Access in another application. For example, all your data may be stored in an Excel or Lotus 1-2-3 worksheet. Rather than retyping all that data, you can *import* the data into Access. Or you may want to use the data you stored in Access in a statistical analysis package that uses Excel files. You can *export* the data to an Excel .xls file.

Using an Access object in another database or program

If you need to use an object from one database in another database, you can easily export the object to another file. Using the same technique, you can export an object from an Access database to a file that isn't an Access file — a dBase or Excel file, for example. You can also use this technique to create a static HTML file. To create a dynamic HTML page that reflects the current contents of the database, create a Data Access Page. *See also* "Adding a Data Access Page to Your Report" in Part VI.

To export an object, follow these steps:

1. Open the database that contains the object.

2. Select the object in the Database window.

3. Choose File⇨Export, or right-click the object and then choose Export from the shortcut menu. Access displays the Export dialog box.

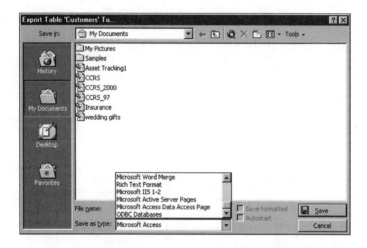

4. Select the file type that you want to create using the Save as Type drop-down list.

5. Select the file to which you want to save the object by typing the name in the File Name box. You can save to a file that already exists, or you can create a completely new file by typing a new name in the File Name box. If you're creating a non-Access file, type a name for your brand-new file.

6. Click the Save button. If you're exporting to a file type other than an Access database, the object is exported.

If you're exporting an existing Access file, you see the Export dialog box, where you can rename the object (if you want to) and tell Access whether you want to export all the data or just the object definition (field names, format, and any expressions).

When you save a report to HTML, Access will ask you for the name of the HTML template file. You can find out about HTML template files from the Access Help system.

Access quietly completes the export process.

To see whether the operation worked, open the file to which you exported the object.

Moving data from Excel

If you have data in Excel that you want to move into a new table in your database, there's a very convenient way to do it — here's how:

1. Display the Tables view of the Database window.

2. Open the workbook that contains your data in Excel. Make sure the first row of data will make adequate field names (you can always change them later — *see* "Renaming a Field" in this part).

3. Select the data in Excel and press Ctrl+C to copy the data to the clipboard.

4. Return to the Table view of the Database window in Access and press Ctrl+V to paste the data into a new table.

5. When Access asks if the first row of your data contains column headings click Yes.

Access creates a new table with the Excel data with the same name that the Excel worksheet that contained the data. You may need to rename your table, but wasn't that easy? *See* "Changing the Name of An Object" in Part II.

Importing or linking to data from an outside source

You can use data from an existing file in two ways: Import it or link to it. *Importing* means bringing the data into your database — as if you'd typed all the data into Access yourself, but without the work. *Linking* means that Access goes back to that other file to find the data each time you need it. You can change the data in the other file and see the changes reflected in your database.

The easiest way to import or link data is to use the Import Data Wizard or the Link Table Wizard. These wizards enable you to see what you're working with and give you more options than importing or linking with a simple menu command. The wizards know how to deal with multiple worksheets in an Excel file, for example. You can even choose to import only selected parts of the data.

Open the database that you want to add the imported or linked data to, and follow these steps to import or link data:

1. Click New in the Tables tab of the Database window and choose Import Table or Link Table from the New Table dialog box.

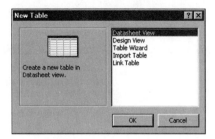

Access displays the Import or Link dialog box, where you specify the name of the file that contains the data you're importing or linking to.

2. Use the Files of type drop-down menu to choose the file type that you're importing from.

For example, if you're importing data from an Excel file, choose Microsoft Excel (*.xls). Access then displays the Excel files in the current folder.

3. Navigate the folder structure (if necessary) to find the file that contains the data you want to use . Click the file name so that it appears in the File name box on the Import or Link dialog box.

4. Click either the Import button or the Link button — the Import button if you're importing data, the Link button if you're linking data. (The name of the button depends on whether you chose Import Data or Link Data in Step 1).

5. The appropriate wizard takes over and guides you through the process of choosing the data you want to import or link to. The windows you see depend on the type of file that contains the data you're importing or linking to.

Undoing

Building a database requires a great deal of experimentation — and sometimes, you try something that you wish you hadn't. That's the perfect opportunity to use the Undo button, which undoes the last action that you performed. When you move the mouse pointer to the Undo button, it gives you a hint about what that last thing was. Undo Typing, for example, indicates that when you click the Undo button, Access undoes the typing that you just entered.

You can click the Undo button more than once to undo more than one action.

Instead of clicking the Undo button, you can choose Edit⇨Undo, or press Ctrl+Z.

Techie Talk

cell: The intersection of a row and a column in a datasheet. A cell holds the information in one field for one record.

click: To move the mouse pointer to something and press the left mouse button.

control: Any object that appears in a report or form. A control can be a line, text, or something that tells Access to display data from a field in a table or query.

cursor: The marker that tells you where you are on-screen. The cursor is usually a thin vertical black bar, although it can be other shapes.

data: Information such as numbers, addresses, dates, and text.

Data Access Pages: Similar to forms, they present data and allow the user to edit existing data and enter new records via Internet Explorer 5 on an intranet or the Internet.

database: An organized collection of data. In Access, a database is a file on your hard disk (or wherever you store it) consisting of tables that contain your data and any other objects you have defined (such as queries, reports, or forms).

default: A suggested setting. In a dialog box, the default setting is the one that Access uses unless you tell it to use something different.

dialog box: A box of options that Access uses to collect information from you.

double-click: To move the mouse pointer to something and press the left mouse button twice in quick succession. You must be careful not to move the mouse pointer between clicks.

drag-and-drop: A method of moving items from one place on-screen to another. To drag and drop an item, move the mouse pointer to the item, press the left mouse button, move the item to the new position, and release the mouse button.

drop-down menu/list: A list of options you can choose from.

dynaset: The data that results from a query. A dynaset is usually displayed in Datasheet view.

field: A category of data in your database. Each field in your database stores one kind of data. You may have a field called Last Name, for example, to store the last names of all the people in a table. In a table, fields are the columns.

font: A style of type. A font is made up of letters and other characters.

footer: Text or other information that appears at the bottom of each printed page.

header: Text or other information that appears at the top of each printed page.

hot key: The underlined letter on a button or in a menu command. You can press the Alt key in combination with the hot key to perform the command without using the mouse.

mouse pointer: The thing (usually an arrow) on-screen that moves when you move the mouse.

object: Part of an Access database. The types of objects that make up an Access database are tables, reports, queries, forms, pages, macros, and modules.

primary key: The field that uniquely identifies each record in a table.

query: The tool you use to get information from your database. You can use a query to select particular records from the database and to create summary calculations, as well as to delete or change records, or make a new table.

radio button: A circle, usually in a dialog box, that shows whether an option is chosen. A dot in a radio button indicates the chosen option. Radio buttons come in groups, and you can choose only one button in the group at a time. To turn off one choice, click another radio button in the same group.

record: A group of fields of related information. One record may consist of a person's name, address, and other information that you want to store. In a table, records are the rows.

right-click: To move the mouse pointer to something and press the right mouse button.

scroll: To view more information on-screen by using the scroll bars, arrow keys, PgUp and PgDn keys, or other navigation keys.

select: To choose. The easiest way to select something is to click it. Selected items are usually highlighted. Occasionally (depending on what is selected), you may have to click at the beginning of the item you want to select and drag the mouse pointer to the end.

shortcut menu: The menu that appears when you right-click. Shortcut menus give you a way to quickly find commands relevant to the task you're working on.

taskbar: The Windows feature that displays a button for each program running. The taskbar usually appears on the bottom edge of the screen, although you can move it to any edge. To use the taskbar, click the button for the program you want to display.

toggle: A key or option that switches between two or more settings. To cycle through the possibilities of a toggle option, click the option or press the key. For example, the Insert key is a toggle option — press the key once to change to overstrike mode; press it again to return to insert mode.

toolbar: The row of buttons below the menu.

toolbox: The box of buttons used for building forms and reports. The toolbox contains a button for each type of object commonly used in a form or report.

VCR buttons: Buttons that look like the ones on a VCR, which help you navigate around an object.

wizards: Access tools that lead you step-by-step through a task by asking questions. The Query Wizard, for example, asks you questions and then builds a query based on your answers.

Index

• **G** •

• **H** •

• R •

• S •

• U •

• V •

• W, Y, Z •

Dummies Books™
Bestsellers on Every Topic!

🧑‍🎓 GENERAL INTEREST TITLES

NESS & PERSONAL FINANCE

Title	Author	ISBN	Price
ounting For Dummies®	John A. Tracy, CPA	0-7645-5014-4	$19.99 US/$27.99 CAN
siness Plans For Dummies®	Paul Tiffany, Ph.D. & Steven D. Peterson, Ph.D.	1-56884-868-4	$19.99 US/$27.99 CAN
iness Writing For Dummies®	Sheryl Lindsell-Roberts	0-7645-5134-5	$16.99 US/$27.99 CAN
sulting For Dummies®	Bob Nelson & Peter Economy	0-7645-5034-9	$19.99 US/$27.99 CAN
tomer Service For Dummies®, 2nd Edition	Karen Leland & Keith Bailey	0-7645-5209-0	$19.99 US/$27.99 CAN
nchising For Dummies®	Dave Thomas & Michael Seid	0-7645-5160-4	$19.99 US/$27.99 CAN
tting Results For Dummies®	Mark H. McCormack	0-7645-5205-8	$19.99 US/$27.99 CAN
me Buying For Dummies®	Eric Tyson, MBA & Ray Brown	1-56884-385-2	$16.99 US/$24.99 CAN
use Selling For Dummies®	Eric Tyson, MBA & Ray Brown	0-7645-5038-1	$16.99 US/$24.99 CAN
nan Resources Kit For Dummies®	Max Messmer	0-7645-5131-0	$19.99 US/$27.99 CAN
esting For Dummies®, 2nd Edition	Eric Tyson, MBA	0-7645-5162-0	$19.99 US/$27.99 CAN
v For Dummies®	John Ventura	1-56884-860-9	$19.99 US/$27.99 CAN
dership For Dummies®	Marshall Loeb & Steven Kindel	0-7645-5176-0	$19.99 US/$27.99 CAN
naging For Dummies®	Bob Nelson & Peter Economy	1-56884-858-7	$19.99 US/$27.99 CAN
rketing For Dummies®	Alexander Hiam	1-56884-699-1	$19.99 US/$27.99 CAN
tual Funds For Dummies®, 2nd Edition	Eric Tyson, MBA	0-7645-5112-4	$19.99 US/$27.99 CAN
gotiating For Dummies®	Michael C. Donaldson & Mimi Donaldson	1-56884-867-6	$19.99 US/$27.99 CAN
sonal Finance For Dummies®, 2nd Edition	Eric Tyson, MBA	0-7645-5013-6	$19.99 US/$27.99 CAN
sonal Finance For Dummies® For Canadians	Eric Tyson, MBA & Tony Martin	1-56884-378-X	$19.99 US/$27.99 CAN
lic Speaking For Dummies®	Malcolm Kushner	0-7645-5159-0	$16.99 US/$24.99 CAN
es Closing For Dummies®	Tom Hopkins	0-7645-5063-2	$14.99 US/$21.99 CAN
es Prospecting For Dummies®	Tom Hopkins	0-7645-5066-7	$14.99 US/$21.99 CAN
ing For Dummies®	Tom Hopkins	1-56884-389-5	$16.99 US/$24.99 CAN
all Business For Dummies®	Eric Tyson, MBA & Jim Schell	0-7645-5094-2	$19.99 US/$27.99 CAN
all Business Kit For Dummies®	Richard D. Harroch	0-7645-5093-4	$24.99 US/$34.99 CAN
es 2000 For Dummies®	Eric Tyson & David J. Silverman	0-7645-5206-6	$14.99 US/$21.99 CAN
e Management For Dummies®, 2nd Edition	Jeffrey J. Mayer	0-7645-5145-0	$19.99 US/$27.99 CAN
ting Business Letters For Dummies®	Sheryl Lindsell-Roberts	0-7645-5207-4	$16.99 US/$24.99 CAN

TECHNOLOGY TITLES 🧑‍💻

RNET/ONLINE

Title	Author	ISBN	Price
erica Online® For Dummies®, 5th Edition	John Kaufeld	0-7645-0502-5	$19.99 US/$27.99 CAN
king Online Dummies®	Paul Murphy	0-7645-0458-4	$24.99 US/$34.99 CAN
™ For Dummies®	Roland Warner	0-7645-0582-3	$19.99 US/$27.99 CAN
ail For Dummies®, 2nd Edition	John R. Levine, Carol Baroudi, & Arnold Reinhold	0-7645-0131-3	$24.99 US/$34.99 CAN
ealogy Online For Dummies®	Matthew L. Helm & April Leah Helm	0-7645-0377-4	$24.99 US/$34.99 CAN
rnet Directory For Dummies®, 3rd Edition	Brad Hill	0-7645-0558-2	$24.99 US/$34.99 CAN
rnet Auctions For Dummies®	Greg Holden	0-7645-0578-9	$24.99 US/$34.99 CAN
rnet Explorer 5 For Windows® For Dummies®	Doug Lowe	0-7645-0455-X	$19.99 US/$28.99 CAN
sting Online For Dummies®	Kathleen Sindell, Ph.D,	0-7645-0509-X	$24.99 US/$34.99 CAN
Searching Online For Dummies®	Pam Dixon	0-7645-0673-0	$24.99 US/$34.99 CAN
sting Online For Dummies®, 2nd Edition	Kathleen Sindell, Ph.D.	0-7645-0509-2	$24.99 US/$34.99 CAN
el Planning Online For Dummies®, 2nd Edition	Noah Vadnai	0-7645-0438-X	$24.99 US/$34.99 CAN
ld Wide Web Searching For Dummies®, 2nd Ed.	Brad Hill	0-7645-0264-6	$24.99 US/$34.99 CAN
oo!® For Dummies®	Brad Hill	0-7645-0582-3	$19.99 US/$27.99 CAN

ATING SYSTEMS

Title	Author	ISBN	Price
For Dummies®, 3rd Edition	Dan Gookin	0-7645-0361-8	$19.99 US/$27.99 CAN
ME For Linux® For Dummies®	David B. Busch	0-7645-0650-1	$24.99 US/$37.99 CAN
IX® For Dummies®, 2nd Edition	John Hall, Craig Witherspoon, & Coletta Witherspoon	0-7645-0421-5	$24.99 US/$34.99 CAN
OS 8.5 For Dummies®	Bob LeVitus	0-7645-0397-9	$19.99 US/$28.99 CAN
Hat® Linux® For Dummies®	Jon "maddog" Hall	0-7645-0663-3	$24.99 US/$37.99 CAN
ll Business Windows® 98 For Dummies®	Stephen Nelson	0-7645-0425-8	$24.99 US/$34.99 CAN
® For Dummies®, 4th Edition	John R. Levine & Margaret Levine Young	0-7645-0419-3	$19.99 US/$27.99 CAN
dows 95 For Dummies®, 2nd Edition	Andy Rathbone	0-7645-0180-1	$19.99 US/$27.99 CAN
dows 98 For Dummies®	Andy Rathbone	0-7645-0261-1	$19.99 US/$27.99 CAN
dows 2000 For Dummies®	Andy Rathbone	0-7645-0641-2	$19.99 US/$29.99 CAN
dows 2000 Server For Dummies®	Ed Tittle	0-7645-0341-3	$24.99 US/$37.99 CAN

Dummies Books™
Bestsellers on Every Topic!

 ## GENERAL INTEREST TITLES

FOOD & BEVERAGE/ENTERTAINING

Bartending For Dummies®	Ray Foley	0-7645-5051-9	$14.99 US/$21.99
Cooking For Dummies®	Bryan Miller & Marie Rama	0-7645-5002-0	$19.99 US/$27.99
Entertaining For Dummies®	Suzanne Williamson with Linda Smith	0-7645-5027-6	$19.99 US/$27.99
Gourmet Cooking For Dummies®	Charlie Trotter	0-7645-5029-2	$19.99 US/$27.99
Grilling For Dummies®	Marie Rama & John Mariani	0-7645-5076-4	$19.99 US/$27.99
Italian Cooking For Dummies®	Cesare Casella & Jack Bishop	0-7645-5098-5	$19.99 US/$27.99
Mexican Cooking For Dummies®	Mary Sue Miliken & Susan Feniger	0-7645-5169-8	$19.99 US/$27.99
Quick & Healthy Cooking For Dummies®	Lynn Fischer	0-7645-5214-7	$19.99 US/$27.99
Wine For Dummies®, 2ⁿᵈ Edition	Ed McCarthy & Mary Ewing-Mulligan	0-7645-5114-0	$19.99 US/$27.99

SPORTS

Baseball For Dummies®, 2nd Edition	Joe Morgan with Richard Lally	0-7645-5234-1	$19.99 US/$27.99
Golf For Dummies®, 2nd Edition	Gary McCord	0-7645-5146-9	$19.99 US/$27.99
Fly Fishing For Dummies®	Peter Kaminsky	0-7645-5073-X	$19.99 US/$27.99
Football For Dummies®	Howie Long with John Czarnecki	0-7645-5054-3	$19.99 US/$27.99
Hockey For Dummies®	John Davidson with John Steinbreder	0-7645-5045-4	$19.99 US/$27.99
NASCAR For Dummies®	Mark Martin	0-7645-5219-8	$19.99 US/$27.99
Tennis For Dummies®	Patrick McEnroe with Peter Bodo	0-7645-5087-X	$19.99 US/$27.99

HOME & GARDEN

Annuals For Dummies®	Bill Marken & NGA	0-7645-5056-X	$16.99 US/$24.99
Container Gardening For Dummies®	Bill Marken & NGA	0-7645-5057-8	$16.99 US/$24.99
Decks & Patios For Dummies®	Robert J. Beckstrom & NGA	0-7645-5075-6	$16.99 US/$24.99
Flowering Bulbs For Dummies®	Judy Glattstein & NGA	0-7645-5103-5	$16.99 US/$24.99
Gardening For Dummies®, 2ⁿᵈ Edition	Michael MacCaskey & NGA	0-7645-5130-2	$16.99 US/$24.99
Herb Gardening For Dummies®	NGA	0-7645-5200-7	$16.99 US/$24.99
Home Improvement For Dummies®	Gene & Katie Hamilton & the Editors of HouseNet, Inc.	0-7645-5005-5	$19.99 US/$26.99
Houseplants For Dummies®	Larry Hodgson & NGA	0-7645-5102-7	$16.99 US/$24.99
Painting and Wallpapering For Dummies®	Gene Hamilton	0-7645-5150-7	$16.99 US/$24.99
Perennials For Dummies®	Marcia Tatroe & NGA	0-7645-5030-6	$16.99 US/$24.99
Roses For Dummies®, 2ⁿᵈ Edition	Lance Walheim	0-7645-5202-3	$16.99 US/$24.99
Trees and Shrubs For Dummies®	Ann Whitman & NGA	0-7645-5203-1	$16.99 US/$24.99
Vegetable Gardening For Dummies®	Charlie Nardozzi & NGA	0-7645-5129-9	$16.99 US/$24.99

TECHNOLOGY TITLES

WEB DESIGN & PUBLISHING

Active Server Pages For Dummies®, 2ⁿᵈ Edition	Bill Hatfield	0-7645-0603-X	$24.99 US/$37.99
Cold Fusion 4 For Dummies®	Alexis Gutzman	0-7645-0604-8	$24.99 US/$37.99
Creating Web Pages For Dummies®, 4ᵗʰ Edition	Bud Smith & Arthur Bebak	0-7645-0504-1	$24.99 US/$34.99
Dreamweaver™ For Dummies®	Janine Warner	0-7645-0423-1	$24.99 US/$34.99
FrontPage® 2000 For Dummies®	Asha Dornfest	0-7645-0423-1	$24.99 US/$34.99
HTML 4 For Dummies®, 2ⁿᵈ Edition	Ed Tittel & Stephen Nelson James	0-7645-0572-6	$24.99 US/$34.99
Java™ For Dummies®, 2ⁿᵈ Edition	Aaron E. Walsh	0-7645-0140-2	$24.99 US/$34.99
PageMill™ 2 For Dummies®	Deke McClelland & John San Filippo	0-7645-0028-7	$24.99 US/$34.99
XML™ For Dummies®	Ed Tittel	0-7645-0692-7	$24.99 US/$37.99

DESKTOP PUBLISHING GRAPHICS/MULTIMEDIA

Adobe® In Design™ For Dummies®	Deke McClelland	0-7645-0599-8	$19.99 US/$27.99
CorelDRAW™ 9 For Dummies®	Deke McClelland	0-7645-0523-8	$19.99 US/$27.99
Desktop Publishing and Design For Dummies®	Roger C. Parker	1-56884-234-1	$19.99 US/$27.99
Digital Photography For Dummies®, 3ʳᵈ Edition	Julie Adair King	0-7645-0646-3	$24.99 US/$37.99
Microsoft® Publisher 98 For Dummies®	Jim McCarter	0-7645-0395-2	$19.99 US/$27.99
Visio 2000 For Dummies®	Debbie Walkowski	0-7645-0635-8	$19.99 US/$29.99

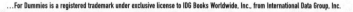

Discover Dummies Online!

The Dummies Web Site is your fun and friendly online resource for the latest information about *For Dummies* books and your favorite topics. The Web site is the place to communicate with us, exchange ideas with other *For Dummies* readers, chat with authors, and have fun!

Ten Fun and Useful Things You Can Do at www.dummies.com

1. Win free *For Dummies* books and more!
2. Register your book and be entered in a prize drawing.
3. Meet your favorite authors through the Hungry Minds Author Chat Series.
4. Exchange helpful information with other *For Dummies* readers.
5. Discover other great *For Dummies* books you must have!
6. Purchase Dummieswear exclusively from our Web site.
7. Buy *For Dummies* books online.
8. Talk to us. Make comments, ask questions, get answers!
9. Download free software.
10. Find additional useful resources from authors.

Link directly to these ten fun and useful things at **www.dummies.com/10useful**

For other technology titles from Hungry Minds, go to
www.hungryminds.com

Not on the Web yet? It's easy to get started with *Dummies 101: The Internet For Windows 98* or *The Internet For Dummies* at local retailers everywhere.

Find other *For Dummies* books on these topics:

Business • Career • Databases • Food & Beverage • Games • Gardening
Graphics • Hardware • Health & Fitness • Internet and the World Wide Web
Networking • Office Suites • Operating Systems • Personal Finance • Pets
Programming • Recreation • Sports • Spreadsheets • Teacher Resources
Test Prep • Word Processing

Hungry Minds™

FOR DUMMIES
BOOK REGISTRATION

Register
This Book
and Win!

We want to hear from you!

Visit **dummies.com** to register this book and tell us how you liked it!

✔ Get entered in our monthly prize giveaway.

✔ Give us feedback about this book — tell us what you like best, what you like least, or maybe what you'd like to ask the author and us to change!

✔ Let us know any other *For Dummies* topics that interest you.

Your feedback helps us determine what books to publish, tells us what coverage to add as we revise our books, and lets us know whether we're meeting your needs as a *For Dummies* reader. You're our most valuable resource, and what you have to say is important to us!

Not on the Web yet? It's easy to get started with *Dummies 101: The Internet For Windows 98* or *The Internet For Dummies* at local retailers everywhere.

Or let us know what you think by sending us a letter at the following address:

For Dummies Book Registration
Dummies Press
10475 Crosspoint Blvd.
Indianapolis, IN 46256

™

BESTSELLING
BOOK SERIES